TELECOMMUTING:

Managing off-site staff for small business

TELECOMMUTING:
Managing off-site staff for small business

Lin Grensing-Pophal

Self-Counsel Press
(a division of)
International Self-Counsel Press Ltd.

Self-Counsel Press acknowledges the financial support of the Government of Canada through the Book Publishing Industry Development Program (BPIDP) for our publishing activities.

Printed in Canada

First edition: 2001

Canadian Cataloguing in Publication Data

Grensing-Pophal, Lin, 1959 -
Telecommuting (Self-counsel business series)

ISBN 1-55180-308-9

1. Telecommuting. I. Title. II. Series.
HD2336.3.G73 2001 331.25 C00-910731-2

The table on page 35 and the "University of Michigan Telecommuting Guidelines" on page 80 are reprinted with permission of the University of Michigan. The "Furniture, Equipment, and Supplies Checklist" on page 42 is reprinted with permission of Smart Valley Inc. The "Telecommuting Safety Checklist" on pages 43-45 and the "Telecommuting Agreement" on pages 183-186 are reprinted with permission of the US Office of Personnel Management. "Managing Telecommuters: Tips for Supervisors" on page 153 is reprinted with permission of the University of Houston — Health Science Center. The safety guidelines on pages 46-47, the "Teleworker Category Matrix" on page 59, "Teleworking Issues" on pages 151-152, and the "Telecommuting Policy" on pages 171-180 are reprinted with permission of AG Communication Systems. Jim Miller's "Prescription for Implementing Telework" on page 49 is reprinted with permission of US West. The self-assessment on pages 75-77 and "Common Traits of Successful Telecommuters" on pages 79-80 are reprinted with permission from *101 Tips for Telecommuters* by Debra A. Dinnocenzo (Berrett-Koehler Publishers, Inc.). The "Telecommuting Project Manager" job posting on pages 95-97 is reprinted with permission of Turner Consulting Group. The "Briefing Session for Prospective Telecommuters" on pages 116-117 is reprinted with permission of Gil Gordon Associates. The "Supervisor's Checklist for Telecommuters" on page 122 and the "Telecommuter's Agreement" on pages 181-182 are reprinted with permission of the California Department of Personnel Administration. The section from "Moving Telecommuting Forward: An Examination of Organizational Variables" on pages 163-165 is reprinted with permission of the New Jersey Institute of Technology.

Self-Counsel Press
(a division of)
International Self-Counsel Press Ltd.

1481 Charlotte Road
North Vancouver, BC V7J 1H1
Canada

1704 N. State Street
Bellingham, Washington 98225
USA

CONTENTS

Foreword xi

Introduction xv

1 Telecommuting: What It Is and Why You Need to Know 1

Executive Summary 3

1. The Origins of Telecommuting 5
2. The Terminology of Telecommuting 7
3. The Trend Toward Telecommuting 9
4. The Growth of Telecommuting 11
5. Myths and Misconceptions 14
6. The Drawbacks and Challenges 16
   - 6.1 For employers 16
   - 6.2 For employees 19

7. The Benefits and Rewards 20
7.1 For employers 20
7.2 For employees 22
8. Case Study 24

2 Getting Started 27
Executive Summary 29
1. Which Jobs Are Best for Telework? 31
2. Is Your Business Ready for Telework? 36
3. Handling Resistance from Managers and Employees 37
4. What Resources are Required? 39
4.1 Office equipment and tools 40
4.2 Safety considerations 41
5. The Characteristics of a Successful Program 48
6. Case Study 48

3 Policies and Procedures 53
Executive Summary 55
1. Policy Considerations 57
1.1 Work hours 58
1.2 Work assignments 58
1.3 Evaluation 58
1.4 Salary and benefits 58
1.5 Overtime 60
1.6 Equipment 60
2. Documenting Your Policies and Procedures 60
2.1 Policy statement 60
2.2 Selection criteria 61
2.3 Expectations/responsibilities of telecommuters 62

2.4 Work schedules 62
2.5 Equipment and supplies 63
2.6 Insurance 64
2.7 Employer's right to inspect workplace 64
2.8 Privacy and confidentiality 64
2.9 Performance measurement 65
2.10 Company policies 65
2.11 Termination of the agreement 65
2.12 Employment-at-will disclaimer 65
3. Case Study 66

4 Hiring Existing Staff As Telecommuters 67

Executive Summary 69
1. Telecommuting Is Not for Everyone 72
2. Selection Criteria 73
3. Assessing Telework Candidates 74
4. Traits of Successful Teleworkers 78
5. Perils and Pitfalls 78
5.1 It just doesn't work 78
5.2 It's not fair! 81
5.3 My manager won't let me! 81
6. Case Study 82

5 Recruiting Telecommuters 85

Executive Summary 87
1. The Internet As a Recruiting Tool 90
1.1 Online recruiting sites 91
1.2 Effective online recruiting 94
1.3 Using your own Web site 98
2. Other Sources of Applicants 98

3. Steps in the Hiring Process 99
3.1 Position requirements 100
3.2 Selection criteria 103
3.3 Interviewing telecommuting candidates 104
3.4 References 105
4. Perils and Pitfalls 106
5. Case Study 107
6 Training Telecommuters and Their Managers 109
Executive Summary 111
1. Telecommuter Training 114
1.1 Characteristics of telecommuter training programs 114
1.2 A structure for telecommuter training 115
1.3 Making it real 117
2. Supervisor/Manager Training 118
2.1 An unnerving transition for managers 118
2.2 A structure for supervisory training 119
2.3 Supervisor's checklist 121
3. Team Training 121
4. Training the Rest of the Staff 123
5. After Training 123
6. Tips for Starting Telecommuters 124
7. Case Study 1 125
8. Case Study 2 127
7 Managing Telecommuters 129
Executive Summary 131
1. The Truth about Managing Telecommuters 133
2. Traits of Successful Telecommuter Managers 134

3. Setting Objectives 136
3.1 Establishing job standards 137
3.2 Establishing goals 139
4. Providing Feedback 141
5. Communication 142
5.1 The technology of communication 143
6. Maintaining Involvement 145
7. Motivating Telecommuters 147
8. If the Relationship Doesn't Work 148
9. Additional Tips for Managers of Telecommuters 150
10. Case Study 154
8 Program Outcomes 157
Executive Summary 159
1. Measuring Program Outcomes 161
2. Why Telecommuting Programs Fail 162
3. Case Study 165
Appendixes
1. Telecommuting proposal 169
2. Telecommuting policy 171
3. Telecommuter's agreement 181
4. Telecommuting agreement 183
5. Telecommuting resources 187
Checklists
1. Furniture, equipment, and supplies 42
2. Telecommuting safety 43
3. Supervisor's checklist for telecommuters 122

Samples

1. Prescription for implementing telework 49
2. Common traits of successful telecommuters 79
3. University of Michigan telecommuting guidelines 80
4. Teleworking issues 151
5. Managing telecommuters: Tips for supervisors 153

FOREWORD
by Gil Gordon

There's a wonderful *Dilbert* comic strip in which Dilbert is meeting with the owner of a small business with which Dilbert's firm is forming a strategic alliance. Dilbert comes in with a very thick binder in his hands and tells the other man that the binder contains the procedures his company uses for project management. Dilbert then says, "I guess a small company such as yours is used to flying by the seat of your pants." The small-business owner replies, "Not exactly," prompting Dilbert to ask, "You mean you're flexible?" which draws the reply, "I mean I'm not wearing pants."

When it comes to implementing telecommuting, there is quite a collection of policies, guides, training programs, and all other kinds of resources available in books and on the Web — but most of them are directed at the large organizations that are typical of where telecommuting got its start.

There's nothing wrong with those procedures and manuals — in fact, most of the problems I see when companies try to implement telecommuting arise when they ignore the practices and knowledge that have developed and accumulated in the last 15 years.

The small- to medium-size organization has, unfortunately, been largely ignored in this scenario. As the *Dilbert* comic suggests, smaller firms aren't generally as likely to have those six-inch-thick binders and multi-page policies and procedures. But that doesn't mean the smaller firms don't have the need for the same kind of guidance as do the big firms that prepare those behemoth policies.

That's why this book is such an important resource. It bridges the gap between the unique needs of the smaller-business employer and the knowledge base and resources typically available to much larger firms. There really isn't a great deal of difference in how telecommuting can be used in smaller firms — the difference comes about because smaller firms just don't have the internal staff, the time, and the bureaucratic inclinations that make those immense policies work elsewhere. Smaller businesses need the convenience of a field guide. They need this book.

Having been involved in the field of telecommuting since 1982, I have seen it implemented in virtually every kind of organization — large and small, private sector and public sector, information-intensive and production or service-based, in the US and elsewhere. There are remarkably few differences across this range of firms. The underlying telecommuting concept of selectively decentralizing the office — and the business benefits of doing so — are more universal than most people realize.

This book takes those relatively universal experiences and methods and focuses them exclusively on the needs and characteristics of the smaller (but not necessarily small) organization. Lin Grensing-Pophal has done that exceptionally well — and has also packed the book with a range of checklists, sample forms, dos and don'ts, and other practical, easy-to-use tools that will make your job easier.

Telecommuting is no longer the exclusive province of the Fortune 500 — and I'm not sure that it ever was. Just as the smaller firms make up the core of the North American economy, the smaller firms are where we're seeing the most growth in telecommuting. The reasons are simple: in addition to being less bureaucratic, smaller firms have more immediate needs, faster response times, and a lean staff that makes each person's individual contribution that much more important.

Telecommuting isn't for every job or every employee in a small firm any more than it would be in a large firm. But when used selectively and appropriately, it's a very effective solution to business problems.

You'll find this book to be a well-researched and thorough — yet highly readable and usable — guide to help you decide the best way to implement telecommuting.

Lin Grensing-Pophal has done the entire community of small- and medium-size organizations a great service by tailoring what we know about telecommuting to this sector of our economy. Take advantage of her hard work and start telecommuting!

— Gil Gordon

INTRODUCTION

To business owners who have been struggling to staff positions at every level of their organizations, it certainly comes as no surprise that the labor pool is shrinking. It also comes as no surprise that it is becoming harder and harder to find talented and qualified employees. What may come as a surprise, though, is the impact that these changes may ultimately have on your organization. Think of the growing number of employees who will be eligible for retirement in the near future. The aging of the baby-boomer population may mean that your ability to fill key positions will soon be threatened.

The job market of North America is fast becoming a place in which telecommuting not only makes sense, but may be necessary. Major changes involving demographics, technology, and globalization affect the workforce first, making adaptability a key strategy for success. Consider the following issues, with which any business, large or small, will have to contend.

a. Shrinking Unemployment Rates

In 1999, unemployment rates in the United States reached a low of 4.3 percent — far below the 6 percent that has traditionally been considered the natural rate of unemployment, and the lowest point unemployment has reached in 30 years. While Canadian unemployment rates have been about 4 percentage points higher than in the US since 1992, a study done in late 1999 by Nesbitt Burns' Economics Department indicated that Canada's natural unemployment rate was also falling — reaching a point of 7.5 percent in the 1990s. The study also showed that Alberta, Manitoba, and Saskatchewan were actually operating at better than full employment. While unemployment rates have been rising in Canada, statistics show that a greater proportion of Canadians have jobs. In 1966, when unemployment was low (3.4 percent), only 55 percent of Canadians over the age of 15 considered themselves part of the workforce; by 1989, that had grown to 67 percent, and by 1995 the figure was at 65 percent.

b. The War for Talent

In Canada, as in the United States, the supply of skilled labor is shrinking markedly, particularly in areas such as programming and computer industries.

Employee turnover and the retention of valued employees were major problems for the majority of US businesses in 1999, according to a retention and staffing survey conducted by Manchester Partners International. Fifty-two percent of the 278 companies surveyed said the problem has increased in the past year, with the average turnover rate hovering at 15 percent. The most difficult employees to hold on to are Information Technology (IT) staff, with 50 percent of respondents ranking them in the highest turnover position. Sales, marketing, and customer service ranked second for 47 percent of the companies, and operations and production employees were third. Thirty percent of these companies reported that replacement costs were more than $10,000.

A hiring survey conducted by Management Recruiters International, Inc. (MRI), a subsidiary of CDI Corp., indicates that the demand for mid-level managers, executives, and professionals continues to be high. Just about every major US industry reported critical needs for these levels of employees during the second half of 1999, as shown in the table below:

Printing	73.9%
Telecommunications	72.6%
Retail Trade	70.4%
Pharmaceuticals	59.9%
Construction	59.0%
Information Technology	58.8%
Financial Services	55.3%
Transportation	55.1%
Electronics	50.9%
National Average	50.3%
Insurance	45.8%
Furniture/Fixtures	42.9%
Energy	41.9%
Metals	41.5%
Machinery	39.4%
Health Care	39.4%
Food	38.9%
Agribusiness	38.2%
Lumber	36.4%
Chemicals	34.6%
Textiles	25.9%

Worse, research by Development Dimensions International (DDI), a global workforce and leadership training, staffing, and assessment firm based in Bridgeville, Pennsylvania, indicates that companies are at risk to lose a substantial number of their executives within the next five years. "There are going to be between 40 and 50 percent of general

Development Dimensions International has named the coming managerial shortfall "The Millennium Elephant."

managers eligible for retirement in the next five years," says William Byham, of DDI. "Most companies aren't ready for retirement from anybody because they don't have the backups. There is a tremendous war for talent."

From the late 1960s to about 1980, the workforce grew because of the size of the baby-boomer population (born between 1946 and 1964) and the major entry of women into the workforce. Since that time, numbers have begun to slow and stagnate. Generation X (born between 1960 and 1984) is a much smaller group than their boomer predecessors. Add to this the impact of millions of boomers moving into retirement. The concern is quantitative, but it's also qualitative.

At DDI, the impending managerial shortfall has been named the Millennium Elephant. "We chose that name," says Byham, "because we think the shortfall is going to be a much bigger, longer-lasting problem than the Y2K Millennium Bug."

c. Growing Skills Gap

Many employers are facing a definite skills gap. Fast-paced technological advancements are increasing the demand for highly skilled, well-educated workers. There is growing concern that school systems are not adequately preparing students to fill this gap. An initiative of the Ohio Business Roundtable, the Ohio Department of Education, and ACT, Inc. has documented that only 1 in 14 Ohio high-school seniors is prepared for performing most skilled entry-level jobs in the state. A scientific sample of 14,474 Ohio high-school seniors from 119 schools were given ACT's WorkKeys™ tests in Applied Mathematics, Reading for Information, Applied Technology, and Locating Information. Test results were then compared with the skills and skill levels required for successful performance in specific Ohio occupations, as defined by WorkKeys job profiles. The findings are contained in the report *Knowledge & Know-How: Meeting Ohio's Skill Gap Challenge.* The findings show that—

- Students performed best in the two of the four skill areas most often included in today's high-school curriculum — Applied Mathematics and Reading for Information. The lowest scores came in Applied Technology and Locating Information.
- The skills gap is greatest for science and social service jobs.

- College-bound students tended to earn higher scores than non–college-bound students. For instance, about 70 percent of college-bound students met workplace standards in Applied Mathematics and Reading for Information, but only about one-third of the non–college-bound students fared as well. In Applied Technology and Locating Information, fewer than 30 percent of college-bound students met workplace standards. However, fewer than 11 percent of non–college-bound students did.

- Students in urban schools scored slightly lower than their counterparts in suburban and rural schools. For instance, in Reading for Information, about 60 percent of suburban and rural students met the average skill requirements for 80 percent of available jobs, while these requirements were met by slightly less than half of urban students.

John M. Goff, Ohio Superintendent of Public Instruction, says the initiative's findings underscore a need for academic improvements connected to work experience during the high-school years. "We are not preparing all of our students to meet world-class standards in core academic areas, and too few students graduate prepared for productive work. Our schools must continue to strengthen students' scores in reading, math, and science — and find ways to apply knowledge to real-world situations."

d. Work/Life Characteristics and Needs of Employees

The needs of employees have changed dramatically over the past 30 years. Fueled in part by a rapid increase in the number of women entering the workforce, more and more employees are expecting — and demanding — a balance between the expectations of work and the demands of personal life. No longer can managers tell employees to leave their personal lives at home. Today's managers recognize that what happens at home has a dramatic impact on performance at work — and vice versa.

Record low unemployment is fueling a business trend to help employees balance home and work responsibilities, says Purdue University work/life expert David Thompson.

An online survey conducted by the Washington Post's Web site (www.washingtonpost.com) asked respondents what special privileges would be most appealing to them. Of the 3,400 respondents, the results broke down as follows:

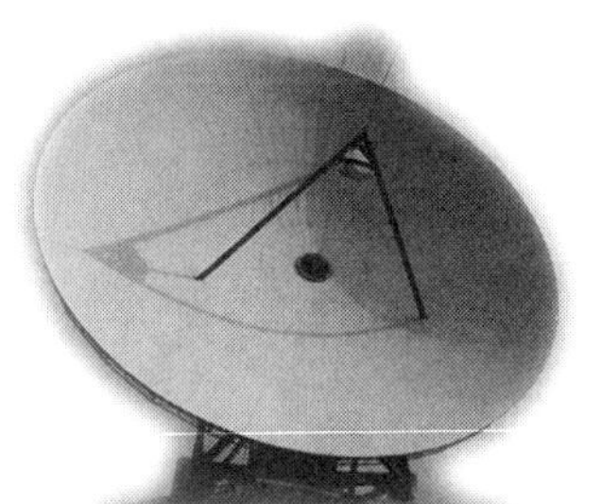

Telecommuting is rapidly gaining popularity as employees try to balance the demands of work and home life. 16 percent of respondents to a Washington Post survey listed telecommuting as the special privilege that would be most appealing to them.

Telecommuting	548
Training/tuition	396
Flextime	379
Benefits	375
Bonus	370
Fitness	357
Money	334
Other perks	302
Time off/vacation	227
Opportunity/growth	109
Recognition/security	80

Recognizing the diverse needs of employees, more companies are offering creative services, from on-site dry cleaning to cafeteria take-home meals, to help boost employee job satisfaction and overall wellness. Thompson says business has learned that a people-friendly and family-friendly workplace can reduce turnover costs, reduce employee stress, and be a strategic weapon in recruiting and retention.

Workers are most likely to be satisfied with their jobs, committed to their employers, and productive at work when they have jobs that offer autonomy, meaning, learning opportunities, support from supervisors, and flexible work arrangements that are responsive to individual needs, according to a comprehensive study of the US workforce released in 1998 by the nationally renowned, nonprofit Families and Work Institute. The study is based on detailed interviews conducted with nearly 3,000 wage and salaried workers in 1997. Service firm Klynveld Peat Marwick Goerdeler (KPMG) was the lead corporate sponsor of the research.

The study indicated that job characteristics and workplace characteristics are far more powerful predictors of employee outcomes on the job than pay and benefits. Job quality and workplace support also had substantial effects on the quality of workers' lives off the job.

"We now better understand how work affects life off the job, and how that in turn affects people's work," says Ellen Galinsky, Institute president and co-author of the report. "Demanding and hectic jobs lead to negative spillover into workers' personal lives, jeopardizing their personal and family well-being. And when workers feel burned out by their jobs, when they don't have the time and energy for their families, these feelings spill back into the workplace, reducing job performance."

"Supportive workplaces offer some protection against this negative fallout from work," says James T. Bond, Institute vice president and principal author of the report. "The more support employees receive on the job — the more flexible their work arrangements and supportive their supervisors — the higher their productivity, the more willing they are to go the extra mile, and the more likely they are to stay with their current employers."

Other key findings from the study include the following:

- *The workforce has changed dramatically.* Today's workforce is more racially and ethnically diverse (20 percent is non-white), older (the median age is nearly 40), and comprised of more women (48 percent is female) than it was 20 years ago. The study also found that higher proportions of workers have college degrees (31 percent) and hold managerial and professional jobs (34 percent).

- *The vast majority (85 percent) of workers have day-to-day family responsibilities at home.* Some 78 percent of married employees have spouses or partners who are also employed, compared to 66 percent in 1977. A full 46 percent of workers have children under 18 who live with them at least half-time. Nearly one in five employed parents is single, and, surprisingly, 27 percent of single parents are men.

- *The roles of married men and women are changing.* Although employed married women spend more time on chores than employed married men do, this gap has narrowed substantially over the last 20 years. On workdays, men spend 2.1 hours on household chores (an increase of nearly one hour) compared to the 2.9 hours (a half-hour decline) women spend. Both men (1.6 hours per workday) and women (1.3 hours per workday) have less personal time.

- *Two-thirds of all employed parents with small children rely on partners and relatives as the primary source of childcare.* When one member of a dual-income couple has to take time off to care for a child, 83 percent of employed mothers say they are more likely to take time off while 22 percent of fathers make this claim.

- *Today's jobs are more demanding than ever.* Employees today spend an average 44 hours per week working — six more than they are scheduled to work. Among employees who work at least 20 hours a week, the hours spent on the job each week have increased an average 3.5 hours (from 43.6 to 47.1) since 1977. In addition, many workers say they have to work very fast (68 percent) and very hard (88 percent). One in three employees brings work home at least once a week, an increase of 10 percent over the last 20 years. The number of employees who would like to work fewer hours rose 17 percentage points over this time period.

- *Many workers experience stress and negative spillover from work.* Nearly one-fourth of all employees often or very often felt nervous or stressed; 13 percent often or very often had difficulty coping with the demands of everyday life; 26 percent often or very often felt emotionally drained by their work; 28 percent often or very often did not have the energy to do things with their families or others; and 36 percent often or very often felt used up at the end of the workday.

- *Some aspects of the job have improved; others have gotten worse.* Workers today have significantly more autonomy and opportunities for learning than they did in 1977, and are more likely to find meaning in their work. On the downside, only 16 percent of workers rate their chances for advancement as excellent, and 61 percent say their chances are fair or poor. And employees today feel far less secure: About three in 10 say it is somewhat or very likely they will lose their jobs within a few years.

- *Family-friendly benefits haven't improved significantly in the last five years.* While 74 percent to 84 percent of employees have access to traditional fringe benefits, only a minority have access to dependent-care benefits such as information and referrals for child care (20 percent) and elder care (25 percent), child-care services (11 percent) or assistance (13 percent), and dependent-care assistance (29 percent). The only significant increase in access to these benefits occurred in the area of elder care.

- *Many workers receive some support and flexibility for their personal or family needs.* Two-thirds of employees can easily take time off during the workday to address family or personal matters. Only half are able to take a few days off to care for sick children without losing pay or vacation time, and 45 percent have some say over their scheduled workday hours. About 19 percent of employees spend at least part of their regular work week working at home. And the vast majority (from 76 percent to 92 percent) feel their immediate supervisors (more so than their workplaces in general) are quite supportive when it comes to their job performance or personal and family needs.

"The bottom line is that employees today are trying to make it work, to restore the balance in their lives," says Galinsky. "Male and female roles are beginning to converge, and children are getting a little more time with their employed parents. But what workers need, what would really make it all come together for them and their employers, is improvement in the quality of jobs and more support in the workplace."

e. Work Ethic and Employee Loyalty

Vault Reports, a New York City–based employment research firm, asked college career-center professionals what they thought employers were looking for in new hires. Topping the list were attributes such as team player, intelligent, and professional demeanor. Finishing nearly dead last, number 10 on a list of 11 items: loyalty.

The massive downsizing that occurred in the 1980s and into the 1990s had a dramatic negative effect on the relationship between employees and employers. Employee loyalty eroded quickly in the face of wage freezes, cuts, and layoffs.

Some would say that the days of loyal employees and employers are gone. There used to be an almost family-like relationship in employment, in which employees and employers looked out for one another. Now, employees are forced to look out for themselves as employers no longer promise a lifetime career.

But recent studies have indicated that employee loyalty is not dead. *Employee Loyalty in America,* a study conducted by The Loyalty Institute of Aon Consulting in Ann Arbor, Michigan, explored the issue of workforce commitment in phone interviews with 2,020 workers selected to be representative of the general working population. The study concluded that employees are basically loyal to their companies.

The issue for employers isn't so much loyalty as it is expectations. The rules have changed. David Stum, director of the study and president of the Loyalty Institute of Aon Consulting, says that in the "new work order," employees will seek short-term social contracts in which employee and employer will outline mutual commitments for each other's success. Such agreements will be individually forged.

Contributing to the change in expectations among employees is the aging of the baby boomer population and the advent of the GenX employee. GenX employees include the 46 million people born between 1960 and 1984. They have been characterized in the media as skeptical and impatient with the status quo, questioning of authority, and fiercely independent. Having witnessed the sacrifices their parents made for their jobs — and the subsequent impacts of staggering job losses in the 1980s and 1990s, they demand a balance between their work lives and home lives.

And they are constantly seeking new experiences. Not content to stay in any one job for a long period of time, they hold an average of nearly nine different jobs by their 30s, according to the US Labor Department. They change jobs in search of new skills, increased responsibility, and new experiences. Their tendency to change positions frequently has had a major impact on the temporary-worker industry.

While clerical and secretarial positions have long been considered typical of temporary positions, this is no longer the case. Today's temporary workers include consultants, executives, highly skilled computer technicians, information-technology specialists, public-relations and marketing experts, office and clerical workers, and even construction workers and day laborers.

Despite record low unemployment and an extremely tight labor market, nearly 300,000 people joined staffing firms as temporary help employees last year, according to a national survey conducted by the National Association of Temporary and Staffing Services. During the fourth quarter of 1998, average daily employment in temporary help services reached 2.9 million jobs, a 10 percent increase from the same period the year before.

Temporary or contract workers are able to move easily in and out of organizations as they work on a variety of constantly changing work assignments, projects, and tasks. The availability of temporary assignments can meet workers' needs for flexibility and allow them to balance school, parenting, or other personal needs.

Thanks to technology such as e-mail and the Internet, employees no longer need to be tied to the workplace. As communications become more flexible, the very nature of work is changing.

f. The Impact of Technology

Technology has had a dramatic influence on the workplace and on the ways in which tasks are accomplished. Electronic mail (e-mail), voice mail, and Internet technology mean that employees can literally be in touch with their employer 24 hours a day, 7 days a week. The 24/7 culture is changing the way that employees and employers interact — it is, in fact, changing the very nature of work.

Under the old system, employees were tied to the workplace. Tools did not exist to allow contact from remote locations. Today, technology is providing both employers and employees with freedom and flexibility that they would never have imagined even ten short years ago.

Technology is allowing employees to question the status quo and challenge the old ways of doing business. "Why do I need to come to the office to work on a report when I can do it at home on my computer?" "Why can't I access voice mail and e-mail from home?" "Why do I have to be physically located in a phone center to answer customer calls? Why can't I be set up from home to do this?"

And because employers are faced with a shrinking labor market and a growing gap between job seekers' skills and employer needs, more and more are responding to these questions with "Why not?"

A study by Deloitte & Touche indicated that nearly 70 percent of the executives surveyed believed that attracting and retaining quality front-line workers will become increasingly difficult by 2005; more than 60 percent expected the same difficulties with executive positions.

What does all this mean? It means that businesses must become more flexible and creative in both the recruitment and retention of employees. It means that the traditional brick-and-mortar workplace will soon give way — in fact, has given way, in many places — to a virtual workplace. It means that neither employees nor employers will be hampered by geographic constraints: an employee can live in Florida and work for a company in Georgia, Wisconsin, California, Ontario, or Saskatchewan.

It means that the era of telecommuting is here to stay, and that it is no longer a luxury; it has become a necessity for companies that want to compete effectively in this new millennium.

Chapter 1
TELECOMMUTING: WHAT IT IS AND WHY YOU NEED TO KNOW

Teleworking: "Any form of substitution of information technologies for work-related travel."

Telecommuting: "Moving the work to the workers instead of moving the workers to work."

— Jack Nilles
(a.k.a. "The father of telecommuting")

Executive Summary

What's the difference between telework and telecommuting?

There is certainly some confusion around these terms and they are often used incorrectly. Telework is a broad term that can be defined as working at a distance. Telecommuting is a form of telework, as are satellite offices, neighborhood work centers, and mobile working.

How common is telecommuting?

Research done for the Information Technology Association of Canada (ITAC) indicated that the number of teleworkers in the US rose to 19.6 million as of mid-year 1999. Telecommuting is common at both large and small companies and for employees in both rural and urban areas. Salespeople, computer professionals, and call center employees were among the first to embrace telecommuting as a work option. But today, employees in just about every profession — line employees, staff employees, and managerial staff — may be candidates for telecommuting.

How many teleworkers will there be in the future?

Predictions vary widely, but it is generally believed that telecommuting will continue to grow exponentially as an option for employees and managers. Telecommuting will be the biggest workplace trend of the 21st century, according to 43 percent of the human resources executives responding to a survey by outplacement firm Challenger, Gray & Christmas. As the labor market continues to shrink and employers are forced to consider new and innovative ways to attract and retain staff, telecommuting is a natural choice.

What is the biggest barrier to telecommuting?

The greatest barrier may very well be attitude. Managers and companies are often hesitant to consider the option because they fear the loss of control when employees are not located in one place. But the reality of today's workforce is dispersion — satellite offices and international firms mean that even employees who aren't considered telecommuters may be located halfway across the world from their coworkers.

TELECOMMUTING: WHAT IT IS AND WHY YOU NEED TO KNOW

1. The Origins of Telecommuting

As long ago as the 19th century, people were telecommuting. While the term wasn't coined until almost 100 years later, the first person on record who performed work at a remote location was a Boston bank president who had a phone line strung from his office to his home — in 1877!

According to Gil Gordon, founder of Gil Gordon Associates, a management consulting firm specializing in the implementation of telecommuting/virtual office and other alternative work arrangements, the terminology may be new, but the concept really isn't. Gordon is recognized internationally as an expert in the virtual-office concept and is a pioneer in the field. "I've heard stories of people working at home in their living rooms with keypunch in the mid 1960s," Gordon says. But, he points out, telecommuting as we know it can be traced to the late 1970s and early 1980s, when more serious attempts at telecommuting were being made by businesses, and we began to see some widespread adoption of the concept.

Telecommuting has been around since 1877, although it did not start to gain widespread popularity until about 100 years later.

Even as early as the 1950s, location was becoming less and less important to the concept of work. Telephone communications were widely established. And as the make-up of work changed to a more information-based economy following World War II, staff could work more independently, without need of constant supervision.

You've heard of the Internet, haven't you? Well, in 1963, a programmer working on the Arpanet Project (the forerunner to today's Internet) withdrew from the project to stay home with his wife, who was going through a difficult pregnancy. Another programmer suggested he install an additional phone line in his home so he could program from there. The practice of working from home still didn't have a name, but people were starting to experiment with it.

In 1973, Jack Nilles, a scientist working on a NASA satellite communications projects in Los Angeles, coined the term telecommuting. Now, Nilles is internationally known as the father of telecommuting. He originally used the term to denote "a geographically dispersed office where workers can work at home on a computer and transmit data and documents to a central office via telephone lines." In 1982, Nilles incorporated JALA International, Inc. (www.jala.com). An international group of management consultants, JALA's mission is "to help organizations make effective use of information technology — telecommunications and computers — and to better cope with the accelerating rate of change in the business environment."

By the time Nilles had come up with a word for the concept of working from locations other than the traditional office, companies were already beginning to experiment with the practice. In 1978, Blue Cross/Blue Shield of South Carolina had started a cottage-keyer project — recognizing that employees could easily perform a number of keyboarding activities at home. In the first year of the project they demonstrated a 26 percent increase in productivity. In 1980, Mountain Bell started a telecommuting project for its managers. That same year the US Army launched a telecommuting pilot.

By the mid-1980s, telecommuting was becoming an increasingly popular option. It seemed to address a number of issues including gridlock, pollution, employee retention, savings on office space — and even increases in productivity.

In 1989, AT&T started a pilot telecommuting program in Los Angeles; the program was expanded to Phoenix in 1990. Employees trialed the idea of working at home several days per month. AT&T's move in this direction was a voluntary response to Title I of the 1990 Clean

Air Act. In 1992, AT&T introduced a formal telework policy and started its Virtual Workplace training programs. By 1999, more than half of AT&T's managers teleworked at least one day a month; 25 percent of their managers teleworked one day or more per week and 10 percent teleworked 100 percent of the time.

Telecommuting was given a boost in 1990 when amendments to the Clean Air Act mandated employer trip-reduction programs. While telecommuting wasn't a requirement under the Act, it was a recommended way to meet trip-reduction goals and a number of organizations began experimenting with this option. The bill was changed in 1995, and reductions in car-commuter trips are no longer mandatory. However, regional or state rules are still in effect, and telecommuting remains one good way to get cars off the road.

There have been some major changes in telecommuting since its early beginnings. These changes have been driven both by demand and by technology — the Internet, e-mail, and cell phones now make it easier than ever to work from virtually any place, at any time.

2. The Terminology of Telecommuting

The term telecommuting is frequently confused with the term telework. Telework is actually a broad term that encompasses telecommuting as well as satellite offices, neighborhood work centers, and mobile working.

Telework means, literally, working from a remote location. The four options mentioned above are all variations of telework.

Telecommuting refers to employees who work at home on occasion or on a regular basis and who are connected to the workplace through various telecommunications links that might include a telephone, electronic mail, or a computer link to office servers. It's the use of information and communication technology to work away from what might be considered the traditional work setting. The most common alternative worksite is the employee's home. Other popular options include telework centers, satellite offices, client offices, hotel rooms, airplanes, trains, and even automobiles.

Satellite offices are facilities that are located at a separate location from the main business headquarters and that house only employees who work for that specific company.

Telework can be done from home offices, satellite offices, neighborhood work centers, or from no fixed location at all.

Neighborhood work centers appear to be exactly like satellite offices, but there is one important distinction. While a satellite office would house employees who all work for the same firm, a neighborhood work center includes employees from a variety of different businesses. Neighborhood work centers are most common in large metropolitan areas and provide space for monthly leasing, as well as business equipment such as fax machines and computers.

Mobile workers are employees who really don't have a specific location where they operate. They may frequently be on the road and may use telecommunications technology to keep in contact with their home office. The most familiar type of mobile worker would be a salesperson.

Another commonly used term is hoteling. Hoteling involves assigning office space to employees who come into the office only occasionally. Rather than being assigned a permanent work area, employees who are hoteling make use of a designated area that they may share with others.

Here are Jack Nilles's definitions of teleworking and telecommuting:

> *Teleworking: Any form of substitution of information technologies (such as telecommunications and computers) for work-related travel.*
>
> *Telecommuting: Moving the work to the workers instead of moving the workers to work; periodic work out of the principal office, one or more days per week either at home or in a telework center. The emphasis here is on reduction or elimination of the daily commute to and from the workplace.*

And, as he points out, since he coined the terms he should know!

Telecommuting is not the all-or-nothing proposition it is often considered. A teleworker is not, necessarily, someone who works from home 5 days a week, 52 weeks a year. In fact, according to the International Telework Association & Council (ITAC), the average number of teleworked days is one to two days per week.

Whether working at a satellite office, in a neighborhood work center, or at home, the concept of telework is dramatically expanding the options available not only to employees, but to employers around the world.

3. The Trend Toward Telecommuting

According to the Information Technology Association of Canada (ITAC), the United States is the leading telework nation. Research conducted for ITAC in 1999 indicates that the number of teleworkers in the US rose to 19.6 million as of mid-year 1999. Of the full-time teleworkers, almost half are employed by small businesses with fewer than 100 employees — 24 percent work for large companies of 1,000 employees or more. Other countries with expanding interest in telework include Canada, Europe, and Japan. According to International Data Corporation's (IDC) 1999 US Residential Telecommunications telephone survey of 1,500 US households, 27.4 percent reported conducting work from home in some capacity — either as telecommuters, corporate after-hours workers, or home-based business operators.

Telecommuting can't happen without the support of businesses, but employees themselves are certainly driving the process. Studies show that more and more companies are offering telecommuting and other flexible options as a means of attracting, retaining, and motivating employees.

The 1999 SHRM (Society for Human Resource Management) Benefits Survey (distributed to 2,500 randomly selected SHRM members), representing responses from 742 human resource professionals, indicates that alternative work schedules are offered by approximately one-quarter of the respondents. A 1999 *Inc. Magazine* survey placed this number even higher — indicating that 53 percent of the responding companies offered telecommuting as an option for employees.

In Canada, service firm Klynveld Peat Marwick Goerdeler (KPMG) surveyed 1,600 large and medium-size companies in the private sector and 425 organizations in the public sector. Among the respondents, 4.5 percent reported always having telecommuters on staff, while another 26 percent reported doing so occasionally. The majority (77 percent) of telecommuters are full-time employees, 13 percent are part-time employees, and the remaining personnel are independent contractors. Although in the past telecommuting may have been initiated in response to employee requests, the organizations themselves seem to have an increasing interest in the practice as a management technique.

Although the main reason for instituting telecommuting is to improve employee lifestyle, another benefit is increased effectiveness in time use.

The majority of those organizations employing telecommuters reported that the practice has increased since 1993, and that they predict increased usage of telecommuting over the next three years.

The KPMG survey showed that telecommuting occurs in almost all areas of the organizations, with telecommuters performing jobs at many levels, from senior management to clerical and administrative roles. Respondents predict the greatest increase in telecommuting will be in the information systems and administration/finance areas in the next three years. In terms of jobs performed by telecommuters, the greatest increases are expected in professional, technical, and middle-management roles.

While the primary reason for instituting telecommuting is to improve employee lifestyle, respondents have discovered the main advantage of telecommuting to be increased effectiveness in the use of time. Cost control and real estate reduction are ranked lowest, both as motivators and as results of telecommuting.

A 1998 study by Ekos Research released during Canada's first Telework Day showed that —

- 55 percent of Canadian employees want to telework now;
- 50 percent feel their jobs are at least partially teleworkable now;
- 29 percent expect to telework next year, and 63 percent expect to telework at some point;
- 43 percent would quit their jobs if another employer offered them an equivalent job allowing telework;
- 33 percent would choose telework over a 10 percent raise; and
- 77 percent believe that new technology facilitates working at home.

The study also indicated that respondents felt that the positive impacts of telework (improved family life, decreased time pressures, more flexible working hours, improved finances) far exceeded any negative aspects. Of the respondents already engaged in telework, the majority spent part of the week at home and part in the office, allowing the opportunity to stay in touch and avoid isolation and loneliness.

Telecommuting as an option for employers and employees has been growing rapidly. The ITAC study shows the recent growth in the number of American telecommuters:

Year	Number of Teleworkers
1997	11 million
1998	15.7 million
1999	19.6 million

In terms of their demographics, ITAC says, telecommuters in 1999 were about 38 years old, 52 percent female, with a median household income of $44,000.

4. The Growth of Telecommuting

Why is there such tremendous growth in telecommuting now? There is a variety of reasons:

(a) *High employment rates.* Employers are finding it increasingly difficult to maintain a fully functioning workforce. The job market is tight and employment is high. Even entry-level service positions have been difficult to fill. In addition, there is a widely publicized skills gap, meaning that employees are not entering the workforce with critical skills that employers need to remain competitive. Telecommuting offers employers the opportunity to draw employees from a much broader market. Hiring telecommuters means that employers are not tied to their own geographic market area — they can recruit and hire from virtually anywhere — expanding dramatically the pool of talent from which they can draw.

(b) *Advanced technologies.* The Internet and personal computers have contributed significantly to the ability of people to work from disparate locations. We now have broadband capacity to homes through cable, satellites, fiber-optics, copper wire, and wireless networks; we have improved electronics and communication devices, mobile phones, palmtops, and portable computers; we have sophisticated voice-mail systems. All of these factors mean that employees can be just as connected to the workplace from their homes — several hundred miles away — as they are from the office around the corner from the boss.

(c) *Reduced costs for office space.* In the United States, the federal government found that it could save money on office space — and attract top-notch workers — by allowing employees to telecommute. In fact, AT&T, a leader in telecommuting, has reported savings of approximately $550 million since 1991 in the elimination or consolidation of office space.

(d) *Employee retention.* In an era of double-income families, it is not uncommon for one spouse to accept a job in another location, requiring the other spouse to leave his or her place of employment. Flexible options like telecommuting allow companies to retain spouses who might otherwise need to change employers as part of their relocation. Telecommuting also allows the retention of employees who have family care needs (either for young children or elderly parents), and employees with disabilities who might be difficult to accommodate in the traditional work setting.

(e) *Traffic patterns.* Congestion is often an issue in metropolitan areas. Major events, in some cities, have led to more employers exploring telecommuting options. When Salt Lake City hosted the Olympics, for instance, preparation for the event meant major road construction and traffic problems. Consequently, a number of employers were more receptive to employees' requests to telecommute. Even in less densely populated areas, travel time can play a role in the move to telecommuting.

(f) *Environmental issues.* One of the early drivers of the concept of telecommuting, particularly in large, metropolitan areas, was the reduction of air emissions and the elimination of pollution. The federal government was an early adopter of telecommuting, and has indicated that about 40 percent of its 800,000 jobs are easily handled by telecommuters. In 1999, 25,000 federal employees were telecommuting. Originally, the program was driven by environmental issues, but additional benefits have helped to sustain the initiative.

(g) *Employer benefits.* Employers are often initially hesitant to allow employees to telecommute, primarily due to concerns that lack of physical presence will denote lack of involvement on the part of the employee. However, those that have allowed employees to work from home have been surprised to find that productivity actually increases, and employees report higher job satisfaction and improved morale. Alongside reduced real estate costs, many companies have also found that their absenteeism and turnover rates have declined after instituting telecommuting programs.

(h) *Employee benefits.* Employees enjoy the flexibility of telecommuting as well as the reduced commuting expenses and hassles. They are better able to balance the demands of home and work; they report reduced stress and higher productivity, and demonstrate a strong sense of loyalty and commitment to those organizations that recognize and respond to their personal needs.

A majority of teleworkers at AT&T report increased productivity due to telecommuting, listing fewer meetings and interruptions as reasons.

Literally thousands of organizations — large and small — have embraced the concept of telework. Some of the companies that have been trailblazers include AT&T, Dun & Bradstreet, Bell South, US West, Merrill Lynch, Lexis-Nexis, Ely Lilly, and Cisco — all members of ITAC's Blue Ribbon Panel (companies considered to have exceptional telework programs).

AT&T adopted a corporate telework policy in 1992. Since then, the percentage of US-based managers who telework has steadily grown to 55 percent, or 36,000 AT&T teleworkers. Of those, 87 percent of managers telecommute an average of six days per month. The remaining 13 percent are in a virtual office arrangement. The majority of AT&T teleworkers report that teleworking has a positive effect on their personal life (74 percent), while only 3 percent report a negative effect. Teleworkers also overwhelmingly report increased productivity (76 percent) when teleworking; only 3 percent report decreased productivity. The top reasons cited for increased productivity were fewer interruptions (70 percent) and fewer meetings (39 percent).

There are many misconceptions surrounding the concept of telecommuting. It's important to investigate these misconceptions with an open mind.

5. Myths and Misconceptions

There are a number of myths and misconceptions associated with telecommuting. Here are a few examples:

Telecommuting is a good idea for women with families, but other employees are unlikely to take advantage of this option.

While telecommuting certainly is a positive option for both women and men with young families and can be a great addition to any company's work/life practices, telecommuting should not be considered a child-care option. Employees of both sexes, with or without families, can benefit from telecommuting.

Employees will be too isolated and will become alienated from the team.

The fear of isolation is an issue for employees; it is also a concern for employers. Isolation may be a misconception, however. A study by Charles Grantham of the Institute for the Study of Distributed Work indicated that virtual office workers spend 43 percent of their time interacting with other workers. Sixty-one percent reported that they contacted their coworkers two or more times a day, and 94 percent checked in three or more times a week.

While there is certainly potential for isolation when employees are working from remote locations and are not physically located near coworkers, isolation is not a certainty. Much can be done to ensure that there is regular and meaningful contact between the telecommuter and other team members.

If an employee wants to telecommute, they'll be out of the office five days a week.

Telecommuting isn't necessarily an all-or-nothing proposition. While some employees do literally work in a remote location eight hours a day, five days a week, arrangements are varied and dependent upon the employee's — and the employer's — unique needs. In fact, according to Telecommute America, a nonprofit organization that promotes telecommuting, telecommuters work an average of only 19.3 hours a week from home.

If I let one employee telecommute, I'll have to let all employees have the opportunity.

Not every job is appropriate for telecommuting and neither is every employee. Jobs, for example, that require frequent face-to-face interaction with internal or external customers are obviously not right for telecommuting. Similarly, employees who require direct supervision, or who have not demonstrated a high level of competency, would not be good candidates for such an arrangement.

The bottom line is that the decision must be made by the company and by the manager. With a telecommuting program you make no guarantees that everyone can be a telecommuter. Part of the process is establishing clear guidelines, standards, and policies.

Everyone will want to telecommute and there will be nobody left in the office.

Just as you may not want certain employees to telecommute, you will have employees who prefer the standard workplace environment. Many employees enjoy the social aspects of work. They like the interactions with others, the opportunity to leave home and enter a different environment. For those people, telecommuting is unlikely to ever become a preferred option. As a manager, you are in control of how you staff your department. There are some managers of workforces comprised entirely of telecommuters — in fact, the manager may be a telecommuter too. There are others who, for whatever reasons, do not find that telecommuting is a viable option. And there are many, many more who find that the right solution is somewhere in between. Ultimately, though, you are responsible for staffing your workforce to provide the optimum service to your internal and external customers.

Only big companies are involved in telecommuting.

Not true. In fact, a survey by Telecommute America showed that 65 percent of the respondents that participated in telecommuting were from companies with fewer than 100 employees. Telecommuting runs the gamut from small firms with only a handful of employees to multinational firms. It's not size that matters, it's process and service.

It is too difficult to manage telecommuters.

In fact, telemanagers and the companies they work for consistently say that good managers are good managers, regardless of whether they're managing someone in the office or from a remote location. The skills are the same.

6. The Drawbacks and Challenges

Even though the time is right for telecommuting, there are a number of drawbacks and challenges of which both organizations and individuals need to be aware.

6.1 For employers

Resistance to change. Telecommuting has been driven largely by employees who, because of their unique personal needs, have requested flexible options for accomplishing their duties. While some employers were early adopters of telecommuting as a work option, and while studies continue to show that more and more companies are offering employees the opportunity to telecommute, many have been resistant to change. Some employers see no need to change a system that has worked for decades and, as most of us can relate to, change can be personally and organizationally challenging.

Out of sight, out of mind. Front-line managers have tended to be the most resistant to the use of telecommuting as an employee option. They believe that employees who are not physically present will be impossible to oversee. "How can I tell whether they're really working?" they ask. "I'm just not comfortable with the idea of letting employees work from home," others say.

Consider, though, how often managers actually oversee the work of their employees in a traditional setting. Managers may be physically located in an area removed from their staff. They may be involved in numerous meetings and other activities throughout the day that preclude direct observation of employees. And, of course, they have their own work to do, meaning that it is very unlikely that they are actually observing employees in the workplace to any great degree.

Abuse of the option. Are there employees who will take advantage of the opportunity to work from home? Employees who may look at telecommuting as a way of saving money and childcare costs while allowing them plenty of time for interaction with the kids? Employees who will spend their time engaged in personal activities instead of concentrating on their assigned work responsibilities? Certainly. But these individuals would be non-productive in any type of setting. A good selection process will serve to screen out these individuals before they are able to take part in a telecommuting program. In addition, careful development of specific — and measurable — goals and objectives can provide management with an objective method of monitoring performance.

Telecommuting raises some interesting legal issues, such as worker's compensation and overtime pay.

Telecommuting demands greater coordination. Companies may be hesitant to start a telecommuting program because they fear that it will demand greater coordination and require more time and effort than the management of traditional staff. This may be true initially as the program is being developed and as the organization is adapting to it. In the long run, however, telecommuting can strengthen all management practices by helping the organization focus more on outcome than process in the management of staff activities.

Telecommuting may have a negative impact on communication. Communication is certainly a challenge when employees are no longer physically located with the majority of their workgroup and when you can't simply walk down the hall to interact. Communication is a challenge in any work setting, however, and as with the coordination of work activities, the communication needs driven by telecommuting may serve to improve communication overall within the organization.

Special communication challenges are not unique to telecommuting. Many companies operate globally today, with employees spread around the world. Communication is an issue that belongs to any organization.

Fortunately, the technology that is now readily available to virtually anyone (at a very reasonable cost) means that distance is no longer relevant.

Legal issues. All employers have legal rights and responsibilities with respect to their employees; telecommuting simply creates different issues. For example, one of the largest areas of concern is for the safety of employees in a home office, or worker's compensation. Another concern that may develop is the one of wage and hour laws (i.e., when will the telecommuter be eligible for overtime pay?).

These are valid concerns and, fortunately, with the growing number of people and companies practicing telecommuting, the vast majority of legal concerns have been explored and tested by someone, someplace, at some time. The two best bits of advice in this area are 1) spend adequate time preparing your telecommuting agreement and include those issues that may create problems, and 2) obtain legal counsel.

Conflict between teleworkers and non-teleworkers. Telecommuting is not appropriate for all people. Your decision on whether or not to allow an employee to telecommute is likely to be based both on the requirements of the job and the individual characteristics of the employee. Working from home or from some other remote location is an attractive option, and it is not unlikely that the employees who are unable to take advantage of it will feel some resentment toward those who are. Conflict may escalate if communication or hand-offs become problematic.

As a manager it is important to remain focused on the business imperatives of the telecommuting decision.

Initial cost of set-up. Some people may be opposed to telecommuting because of concern over the costs involved. Costs will, of course, vary depending on the job that needs to be done, but generally speaking, it should cost no more to set up an employee to work from home than it does to accommodate the employee at the normal work setting. In fact, many companies have documented substantial savings in office space and equipment needs.

Careful planning is the key to controlling costs, as is common sense. A telecommuter may have the need to make photocopies from time to time, but that does not necessarily mean that he or she should be provided with a photocopier for his or her home office.

Negative impact on teamwork. There is something to be said about the camaraderie that develops between a group of people working together, day after day, within the same work environment. And it can certainly be challenging for a manager to build and maintain that same sense of team when some of the team members are seemingly absent. But it can be done.

6.2 For employees

Not all employees are anxious to telecommute. In fact, employees harbor a number of fears about telecommuting. As a manager it is important that you understand some of these concerns and that you're able to directly and candidly discuss them with staff members. There are disadvantages to telecommuting and, for some employees, these disadvantages can be insurmountable.

Employees may be hesitant to try telecommuting, fearing that they may have difficulty advancing in their careers if they are less visible.

Isolation. One of the real benefits of working at the office is the social interaction with other people. While any telecommuter should have ample opportunity for communication with the head office — through e-mail, phone, video conference, and in-person meetings — the fact remains that a lot of time will be spent alone. While some employees may thrive in this type of environment, others may find the isolation difficult to deal with.

Home distractions. People working from their homes often have difficulty creating an appropriate boundary between home and work. Friends, family, and neighbors may perceive that the at-home employee is more receptive to drop-in visits, phone calls, and other interruptions.

Telecommuters whose arrangements allow them to work with their children present have other distractions. And, of course, there are the distractions that telecommuters create for themselves: the temptations of nice, sunny days; the lure of the television; the unrelenting desire to throw in a load of laundry.

Workaholism. On the other hand, the difficulty of drawing a distinction between home and work may create a problem of over-dedication to the job. Telecommuters are often tempted to work longer hours and can find it difficult to create appropriate boundaries between work responsibilities and personal needs. When the office is always just steps away, the lure of completing a project, checking e-mail, or doing just one more thing can be strong.

Limited access to copiers, fax, and other office services. While you will want to carefully consider each telecommuter's needs in terms of work equipment and tools, depending on the employee and his or her job, you may not be able to justify providing every piece of office equipment available for the home office. An employee may need to rely on administrative assistance at the head office or plan occasional trips into the office to take care of routine tasks.

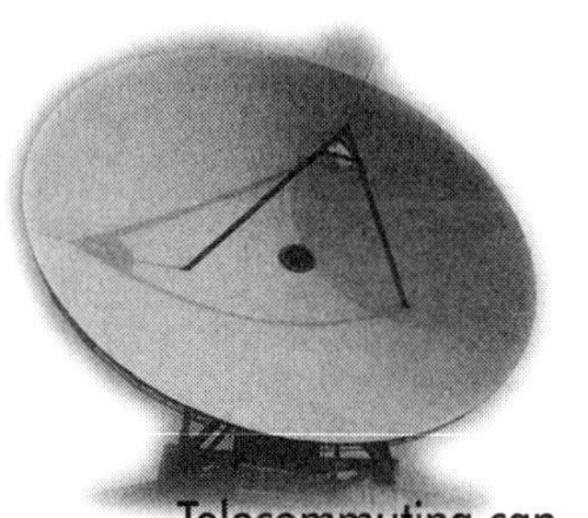

Telecommuting can benefit both employers and employees in a variety of ways.

Invisibility — a career killer? Employees may be hesitant to pursue telecommuting because they have come to view it as a career killer. They fear that if they aren't continually involved, they will be overlooked for key projects, assignments, and promotions. This is a very real concern. However, a 1997 survey of telecommuters showed that 63 percent felt that teleworking had been a positive influence on their careers, and only 3 percent reported any negative impact.

Typically, it is the most independent and self-motivated individuals who are good candidates for telecommuting — the same traits that characterize upwardly mobile employees in general. As a manager, one of your key responsibilities is employee development. Telecommuters, as part of the staff, need to be part of this process.

7. The Benefits and Rewards

Certainly there are potential barriers to making telecommuting work and there are some disadvantages for both employees and employers. There are also, however, a number of very definite advantages; there are good reasons why so many individuals and companies are turning to telecommuting as a work option.

7.1 For employers

Improved productivity. The Gartner Group estimates productivity improvements of from 10 percent to 40 percent. Nortel, with more than 4,000 telecommuters, reports productivity improvements of 24 percent since 1995 — with an associated 10 percent increase in job satisfaction and reduced turnover risk of 24 percent. Surveyed employers also reported productivity gains of approximately $1,850 for each teleworker, per year.

Reduced sick time. Employers find that telecommuters have fewer sick days — an average of one to two days a year. It makes sense. There are times when a cold may make the thought of spending the day at the office seem like torture, but you might be perfectly able to function at home. A telecommuting employee can save an employer up to $10,000 each year in combined absenteeism reduction and job retention costs, according to a survey by the International Telework Association and Council. According to the survey, employers can save 63 percent of the cost of absenteeism per telecommuter or $1,086 per employee per year (based on the average salary reported by teleworkers, $44,000, combined with the average number of days absent on which teleworkers were still able to work from home).

Reduction in office space costs. IBM has reported $75 million in annual savings on real estate expenses because of their telecommuting program. AT&T estimates that its implementation of teleworking results in an average savings of $25 million per year.

Environmental concerns. While the Clean Air Act was changed in 1995 and no longer makes reductions in car-commuter trips mandatory, environmentally aware employers know that telecommuting can have a positive impact on traffic congestion and, ultimately, emissions.

Weather and other traffic-related concerns. In Atlanta, companies began implementing telecommuting during the summer Olympics when traffic related not only to the event, but also to event preparation, created difficulties for commuters. In northern climates, telecommuting means that snow days are a thing of the past. When you have only to commute, on foot, from one room to another in your house, bad weather is no longer a barrier.

Broader talent pool. The labor pool is shrinking. It is more and more difficult to find skilled, qualified, and motivated employees. Telecommuting (and the technology that goes with it) makes it possible to bypass the boundaries of geography. For employers, that means the ability to select from a much broader pool of talent. It also means that barriers are removed when, for instance, a merger means that corporate headquarters moves to a new location and a number of highly skilled employees, unable or unwilling to relocate, now have the option of continuing to work for the company, but from their homes.

Enhanced opportunities for disabled individuals. Telecommuting provides a workable and effective way to accommodate employees with various health problems and disabilities that might otherwise keep them out of the labor market. Far beyond complying with legal regulations, the option of telecommuting can allow employers to provide highly qualified but disabled employees with the opportunity to contribute their talents toward meaningful endeavors.

Improved attractiveness of company to job candidates. Employees are, more than ever, giving their personal lives precedence over their professional lives. To many, the ability to work in a flexible environment is very attractive. Even those employees who are not interested in telecommuting may perceive a company that offers the option as being progressive and concerned with meeting the needs of its employees.

Move toward management by results. All managers should manage like managers of telecommuters. By focusing on results, managers can let go of outmoded ideas of employee surveillance or concern about the number of hours that an employee puts in. What matters are the outcomes. Today's successful managers work collaboratively with their employees, recognizing that the measurement of performance depends more on quantitative results than subjective perceptions of an employee's hard work.

7.2 For employees

Reduced or eliminated commute time. In major metropolitan areas and even in some smaller communities, a daily commute may mean putting up with traffic, congestion, long wait times, and frustration. Telecommuting eliminates these concerns — and allows employees to save money on gasoline, vehicle maintenance, and other travel-related costs. The elimination of a one-hour, round-trip commute each day results in a savings of six full work weeks per year.

Flexibility. Formerly, employees were confined to their work areas from a certain time in the morning until a certain time in the afternoon, for a specific number of days each week. They were generally allowed one break in the morning and one in the afternoon (both at pre-determined times) and a lunch period of anywhere from 15 minutes to an hour. To put it simply, their time was rigidly controlled and governed by the needs (or, more precisely, the whims) of their employers.

As employees have become more independent and the employment options available to them have increased, they have begun to question this rigidity and to request — even demand — flexibility in how their time is scheduled. Telecommuting responds to these requests by recognizing that it is no longer a 9-to-5 world. Today's employees, if provided with the appropriate work tools and communication channels, can effectively work any time during the 24 hour day — 7 days a week.

An environment free of disruptions. The workplace can be very distracting and may result in lost productivity. Telecommuters frequently report (and companies agree) that they are more productive because they have greater privacy and fewer unplanned interruptions of their time.

Ability to balance work and home demands. Telecommuters are better able to balance the demands of work with the demands and personal needs of their home lives. Raising young children, caring for older parents, pursuing hobbies and personal interests; all this can be accomplished with less stress and frustration when the traditional concept of work is changed to one that recognizes the needs of the whole employee.

Decrease in miscellaneous expenses (i.e. clothing, meals). As any employee knows, there are a lot of miscellaneous expenses associated with working, including transportation costs, clothing, and food. Telecommuters are able to save on these costs, which results in a positive impact on their disposable income.

Elimination of transportation problems. Telecommuting eliminates travel concerns for employees in areas where winter can mean snowy and icy roads — and days when they simply can't safely get to work.

Improved morale and job satisfaction. A study done for Telecommute America in 1997 showed that telecommuters were very happy with their jobs. The study asked telecommuters what it would take for them to give up their jobs. Their responses were "double my pay" or "nothing would make me give it up." Two-thirds of the respondents indicated they would not change the way they work at home. They saw themselves as productive and organized professionals.

While the many misconceptions associated with telecommuting can certainly keep companies from moving toward this flexible option, the biggest factor that limits the use of telecommuting at many companies is trust. Embarking on a telecommuting program can require a major paradigm shift for many organizations and individuals. Rather than believing that you are paying an employee for his or her time, you must move to an understanding that you are really paying an employee for his or her output — whether that output is measured in number of sales, completion of specific projects, or consultation.

Telecommuting means that we no longer have to go where the work is. Today, the workplace has become more of a concept than a place.

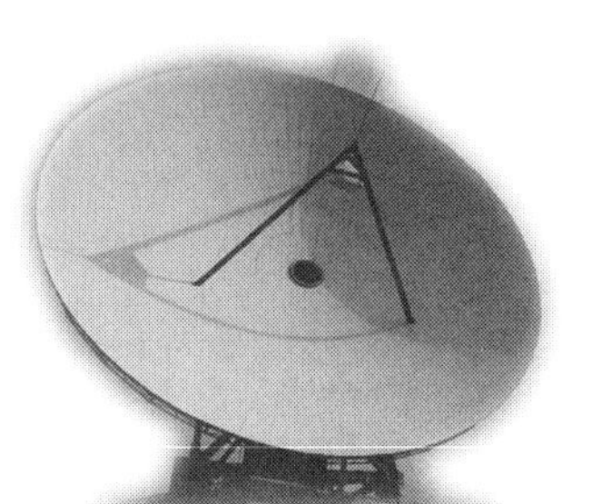

Carol Stein of HR Library successfully convinced management to let her telecommute. She stresses the importance of having "a very precise plan" before requesting or attempting to telecommute.

8. Case Study

When she was hired to run HR Library (www.hrlibrary.com), an Internet research company, Carol Stein was asked to move to Colorado. She saw no need to relocate. Stein approached the management of the firm and said, "This is all Internet based. What difference does it make where you live?" The CEO of HR Library's parent organization considered her question and replied, "Give me a budget." She did.

Stein's plan was approved by her company's board of directors and the rest, as they say, is history. Her creative approach and ability to reframe the traditional business setting has, she says, "given me the opportunity to hire the best and the brightest around the country." HR Library is staffed by librarians with master's degrees in library science who are subject specialists in human resource issues and have expertise in research.

One woman works from a farm in Maine. Stein comments, "The only problem is when the cows get loose and she can't talk to us!" Another works from her home in Kissimmee, Florida. Formerly, her son had a two hour commute to come home from high school; now she takes ten minutes to go pick him up. Yet another HR Library associate lives in a small town in Nebraska, works at another full-time traditional job, but does contract work for HR Library. "These advantages," Stein says, "have a tremendous amount of value" for employees. "I wanted people who were very seasoned," she says, "because I knew I couldn't manage them 24 hours a day, 7 days a week. The people that I found appreciated the opportunity to balance their work and their lives, and they love it."

There is also substantial value for the organization. "It really costs very little to run HR Library," she says. "We don't have any brick-and-mortar. We cover everybody's expenses, but our overhead is negligible, which increases our profit margin." And, she adds, productivity is enhanced in a virtual community. "You're not stuck in meetings, or worrying about how long you can take for lunch, or getting stuck in traffic, or that you have to get the laundry done."

One of the keys to HR Library's success is communication. "My communication has to be awesome," Stein says. "It has to be constant. It has to be precise."

HR Library staff members work a core set of hours — from 8:00 a.m. to 12:00 p.m. — each day, when they are expected to be available to communicate either by phone or online in a chat room setting. Stein said the autonomy was a shock to some of her employees initially. "Other than the core set of hours," she says, "I don't care if they take a three hour lunch break or go to the dentist. I don't care when they work. All I care is that they get their work done when they commit to getting it done. It's a very different work style but it allows individuals, including me, to work when they are at their strongest."

Stein holds an online staff meeting once a week — usually on Monday morning. The group also gets together for face-to-face meetings once a month.

"If anything, you have to over-communicate," Stein says. "You have to be very clear and very concise in what you ask for. And you can't just forget about them. You have to be an excellent communicator. And a lot of managers aren't."

Stein believes that the traits of a strong telemanager mirror the traits of any strong manager, and that having a strong manager is a critical component of any successful telework operation. "In some organizations you can succeed in spite of having a bad manager. In this case, if you don't have a really strong manager, there is no telecommuting organization that will work."

Chapter 2
GETTING STARTED

"You can do any idea you want from anywhere you want with the available technology and the new attitudes people have about collaboration."

— JENNIFER JOHNSON
Founder of virtual agency Johnson & Company

Executive Summary

What types of jobs are best suited for telecommuting?

There are a wide variety of jobs — or portions of jobs — that can be performed by telecommuters. As this option becomes more widespread, more and more companies and their employees are exploring creative ways of offering it. Traditionally, the types of jobs that have been most suited to telecommuting are those that require limited face-to-face contact with coworkers. But today, advances in technology and adjustments in attitude mean that a wide range of people have been able to telecommute effectively.

How much does it cost to establish a telecommuting program?

That depends. It depends upon the type of job being done, the number of people working as telecommuters, and their equipment and communication needs. Costs can vary widely. Hewlett Packard and Pacific Bell have reported average costs per employee of $4,000 to $6,000 per year; but remember, your actual costs will depend on the type of work being done and the equipment and technology needs of your home-based employees.

What is the best response to an employee's request to telecommute?

It is best to consider telecommuting as an option before a request is made by an individual employee. The decision to allow telecommuting should optimally be based upon the needs and characteristics of the job — not the personal needs of the employee. However, many organizations do not consider telecommuting as an option until a valued employee is lost due to relocation. The best response to any request is to carefully consider the impact of telecommuting on the organization and its customers and employees.

Who should be responsible for providing equipment for an employee's use at home?

There are a number of benefits to the employer in providing the equipment that employees will use. Primary among these is control. If it's your equipment, you are able to indicate what type of equipment the employee should have, and to determine how that equipment is used and when it is serviced and upgraded. Employer-owned equipment may also be wise from a safety and security standpoint, particularly if the employee will have access to sensitive customer or company data.

What safety issues should I be concerned about when my employees are working from home?

The Labor Department has indicated that it will issue a formal policy directive stating that it will not hold companies responsible for the safety of telecommuting employees' home offices. But questions remain, and it's clear that this is not an issue that is going to go away. It is best to err on the side of caution by providing employees with clear expectations and guidelines on how to establish a safe working environment at home.

GETTING STARTED

Perhaps you already have a telecommuting program and are looking for ways to make the program more efficient, more effective, or more equitable across the organization. Or maybe an employee has asked you about the option of telecommuting. Or you may simply be considering telecommuting as an option because you've heard so much about it and realize it is probably the way of the future.

Regardless of your motivation, it's best to be proactive rather than reactive. Before an employee surprises you with a proposal, or simply asks, "Can I work from home?" you should have considered the pros and cons and determined what your organization's policies and procedures will be.

1. Which Jobs Are Best for Telework?

There are certain types of jobs that have involved telecommuting for years. Salespeople, for instance, have traditionally operated out of places other than a typical office setting. They may have worked on the road or they may have worked from their homes. Freelance writers for major magazines work from their homes or from remote locations — and are not physically located in the office, or even in the city, where

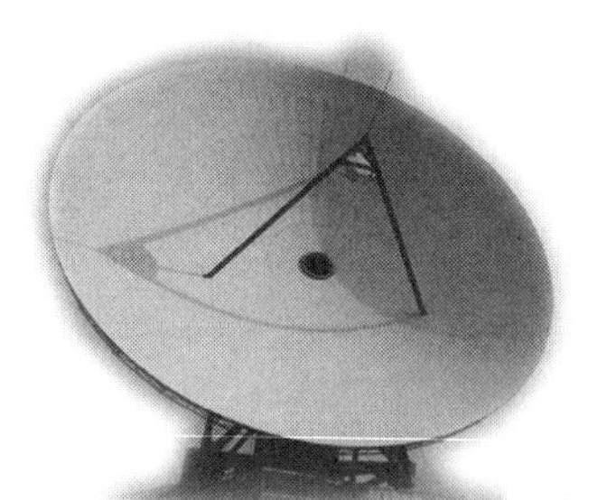

There are a number of factors to consider when deciding whether telecommuting would be appropriate for a particular job.

the magazine is located. Telemarketers often do not require a centralized location, but may operate virtually from their homes or satellite centers. As long as they have the communication equipment and computer information they need to sell the company's products and services, where they sit really doesn't make a difference. And more recently, the computer industry has spawned some major growth in the prevalence and acceptance of telecommuting for a variety of positions.

There are also certain jobs that may require the employee to be physically on-site. Some obvious examples are waiters and waitresses, bank tellers, and check-out clerks in grocery stores or retail settings. With the rapid changes being made in technology and in the way we view work, however, and with some creative solutions, even some of these jobs may eventually be appropriate for telecommuters. A short time ago, most people would have said that teachers could not telecommute — they had to be face-to-face with their students. Today, technology has made it possible for students to take courses online, meaning that the teacher and the students can all be located in different places. Similarly, many people still feel that management positions are not appropriate for telecommuting, yet more and more management staff are telecommuting today.

But what kinds of jobs are most suitable for telework in today's business climate?

TeleCommute Solutions (TCS), a leading turnkey solutions provider for the corporate telecommuting workforce, designs products to help meet the needs of organizations and individuals engaged in telecommuting. TCS suggests five types of work that are most appropriate for telecommuters:

(a) Jobs that involve more telephone interaction than face-to-face interaction. A great many phone centers and telemarketing operations utilize telecommuters; in fact, telephone interactions are probably one of the best examples of a job that is dependent on the availability of technology.

(b) Jobs that can be evaluated primarily by quantitative rather than qualitative results. Results are what count when managing telecommuters — not the amount of time spent in the office. Sales positions are a good example of a type of job in which results dictate success.

(c) Jobs that do not involve high security or handling of proprietary data. Data security is a major issue and is becoming more and more important as technology continues to make the sharing of data easier. In the health-care field, for example, confidentiality of patient information is a major issue.

(d) Information-handling jobs that require computers (i.e., insurance, accounting, programming, data entry, design).

(e) Individual-contributor jobs not dependent on a team environment to accomplish tasks. Examples might include freelance writers, graphic designers, consultants of various types, and, often, computer programmers.

TCS identifies a number of job functions that are suited to telecommuting. These include —

- data entry,
- typing,
- computer programming,
- research,
- writing,
- editing,
- graphic design,
- report preparation and analysis, and
- record keeping.

Of course, there is room for interpretation and flexibility within your own establishment, but the TCS suggestions listed here can form the foundation of any telecommuting program.

The telecommunications giant Sprint has a very formalized process for determining whether or not a position is appropriate for telecommuters. The people at Sprint have created a company handbook that walks managers through the selection process.

Five major areas are considered:

(1) The job itself

(2) The function that the person is performing

(3) The individual's interaction with the workgroup

(4) Space and equipment requirements

(5) Information security requirements

Management is asked to rate each item according to a scale on which **a** meets all the requirements and **e** is not a good selection.

Over time and through experience, Sprint has been able to identify certain types of jobs that fall into each of the categories from **a** to **e**:

(a) Internal audit functions, events management, training and development, processing operations, and outside sales.

(b) Positions that may require technology beyond what a typical user would have in the office — specific positions might include systems developers, programmers, producers, or directors.

(c) Positions that provide support to the organization such as field staff, marketing services, regulatory and government affairs, and some engineering functions.

(d) Positions that Sprint feels are almost impossible to perform away from the workplace, including: human resources, corporate communications, public relations, inside sales, end-user support, customer service, operator service, and safety.

(e) Positions that are considered definitely not appropriate for telecommuting; treasury, procurement, controller and accounting functions, strategic planning and development, law, warehouse distribution, and corporate security.

Remember that these criteria are specific to Sprint. Other organizations may — and often do — consider some of Sprint's category **d** and **e** positions appropriate for telecommuting. The key is to carefully review your organization's needs, your job functions, and the specific criteria that will determine whether a specific position is appropriate to be performed off-site.

At the University of Michigan, categories of "acceptable" and "unacceptable/challenging" are assigned to telecommuting applications as follows:

ACCEPTABLE	UNACCEPTABLE/CHALLENGING
System administration with tasks that can be done remotely.	Anything that requires face-to-face contact with internal or external customers (front-line support).
Technical writing.	Anything that requires hands-on contact with equipment.
Communications development.	Interviewing and performance reviews.
Software development.	Setting final work plans.
Graphic design.	Teaching courses.
Referral consulting.	Projects requiring large amounts of collaboration.
Course development.	Clerical support (i.e., receptionist, file clerk).
Administrative tasks (e-mail, status reports, budgets, etc.)	Hardware-related services.
Web development.	Contract discussions.
Programming.	Staff meetings.
Certain research (i.e., online).	
Individual work (non-collaborative).	
(Copyright© 2001 University of Michigan, Information Technology Division, ITD Telecommuting Task Force — www.itd.umich.edu/telecommuting)	

Be sure to clearly outline company policies on work hours, work assignments, evaluation, salary and benefits, overtime, and equipment.

These methods of assessment may provide a good starting point for your telecommuting program, but you will have to adapt your policy to suit the needs of your business. Don't make your decisions in a vacuum. Involve other members of the organization — and even your customers — in the decision-making process. Developing a dialogue to consider these issues will not only help you make an informed decision, but will ease some of the concerns and misconceptions that other employees and managers may have.

2. Is Your Business Ready for Telework?

Companies in which telecommuting seems to be most successful share a number of characteristics, which are outlined below.

Commitment and support from management. If yours is a small, independently owned business managed primarily by you, you can move forward with a telecommuting program with few problems. The larger your business and the more management staff involved, however, the more work that needs to be done to encourage commitment and support from management. A telecommuting program will not be as effective if it is applied inconsistently throughout the organization — for example, if one manager committed to telecommuting allows employees to work from home, but another refuses to consider the option.

Selection at the department level. Individual managers and supervisors need to be responsible for selecting the positions and individuals most suited to telecommuting. This is part of managing a department. While the rules and criteria should be applied consistently from an overall business level, it is important that actual selection of telecommuting positions and individuals occurs at the department level.

Clear guidelines. Clear guidelines are key. They should be carefully considered, thoroughly documented and communicated, and consistently applied. Chapter 3 provides more detail on developing guidelines and offers sample guidelines and language that can be modified to fit your business needs. The guidelines will indicate to employees and managers what criteria are needed for selecting telecommuters, how to request consideration as a telecommuter, and what the requirements are for ongoing participation.

A comprehensive telecommuting contract. A telecommuting contract ensures that the organization and the telecommuting employee are on the same wavelength when it comes to the nitty-gritty of telecommuting. Items to be included in the contract include hours the employee is expected to be available by phone or e-mail, times the employee will need to report to the office, equipment that will be provided by the employer, safety issues, performance expectations, and training. See Chapter 3 for more information.

Training for both telecommuters and their managers. Training of both telecommuters and their managers is essential. Simply providing an employee with a computer and e-mail is not enough. You may also want to consider providing training for those employees who will still be operating out of the office. The more you can do to thoroughly prepare the individuals involved in your telecommuting activities, the greater your likclihood of having a successful program. Chapter 6 provides detailed information on establishing training programs.

A method of evaluating the program. How will you know your program is successful? Establishing clear criteria to evaluate the success of the program against your pre-determined goals will help you determine if the time and effort invested in telecommuting is truly beneficial for your organization.

3. Handling Resistance from Managers and Employees

Not all of your employees or your managers are going to eagerly embrace the concept of telecommuting. Many employees, particularly those that have been on the job for a number of years and have grown comfortable with a particular way of working, may be threatened by the changes that telecommuting may bring.

The best way to respond to resistance is to understand where the resistance is coming from and what issues are creating concerns. Some of the concerns are predictable and, as we saw in chapter 1, there are a number of myths and misconceptions that you can clarify with employees.

For managers, concerns often center around issues such as—

- "How can I supervise someone who is not in the office?"
- "How will I know if these employees are really working?"

- "Is it worth my time and effort to institute the guidelines and tracking systems necessary to make this work?"

These are legitimate questions, and it is important that you take the time to seriously listen to the concerns of your management staff and work out any problems.

The idea of supervising employees who are not physically accessible can be troublesome to managers who are used to having employees within view at all times. It is a different way of managing, but it is not an insurmountable problem. We will be discussing methods of managing telecommuters in chapter 7.

Another very legitimate concern that managers have about telecommuters is that they will be out of sight, and therefore out of mind. Managers are concerned that employees working from home will miss out on critical information because they are no longer part of the informal communication channel, that their role on the team will be diminished, and their relationships with peers — and managers — will erode. That certainly can happen. Effective communication is a key component of any successful telecommuting role. For more on establishing effective communication with telecommuters, see chapter 7.

Managers aren't the only ones who may be resistant to telecommuting. Employees may also have concerns, and their discontent, if not addressed, can hinder the success of the program. Employee concerns often include—

- "It's not fair that employee X can work from home, but I can't."
- "Employee Y just wants to stay home with the kids."
- "I'm going to have to work harder to pick up the slack for these telecommuters."
- "How am I supposed to share information with people that aren't even around?"

There is an inherent benefit implied in the ability to work from home. Employees who are given this opportunity may elicit envy from their coworkers who, for whatever reasons, are not able to telecommute. It is important to recognize the potential for internal conflict and jealousy. To minimize these conflicts, it is necessary to have very clearly identified, defined, and communicated criteria for the telecommuting program. Consistently adhering to these criteria can help to minimize conflict and jealousy among employees.

Frequent communication is an excellent way to overcome misconceptions that employees may have about their telecommuting peers. The concern that a new mother just wants to spend time at home with the baby, for instance, can be minimized by communicating the goals of the position and sharing information about the attainment of those goals. For example, if a telecommuting employee is part of a workgroup that is responsible for handling insurance claims, holding each employee (telecommuting and traditional) accountable for a specific number of claims can eliminate concerns about how time is being spent at home.

Resistance to change can be most readily overcome by implementing a well-defined system of policies and procedures with which everyone can become quickly familiar.

4. What Resources Are Required?

The cost for setting up a home office for a telecommuter can vary dramatically, as you might imagine. Different jobs will, of course, require different tools, and different companies have different capabilities. Who, then, should supply what? It seems that this, too, varies from business to business. Brad and Debbie Shepp, authors of *The Telecommuter's Handbook* (McGraw-Hill), surveyed 100 telecommuting companies and found that 48 percent supplied all of the necessary equipment for telecommuters. Another 26 percent shared the equipment expense with their telecommuters. Pacific Bell budgeted $4,000 per person, per year, for home-office needs, while Hewlett-Packard's budget ranged from $4,000 to $6,000.

Jim Miller of US West Extended Workplace Solutions is passionate about telecommuting and the benefits it offers to employees and the businesses for which they work. He cautions against buying more technology than is really needed. "Not everybody needs to have high-speed connections from their home to accomplish their tasks. The business has to dictate to the end user. Based upon the work they're going to be doing, you determine the value of the investment that will be made on their behalf. You don't take a sledgehammer to pound in a ten-penny nail."

It is usually best if employers provide the equipment for a home office, but many companies require the telecommuter to supply at least some of the equipment.

Another concern for many organizations may be security. But Miller points out, "Some of the largest financial institutions are the largest users of teleworkers — Merill Lynch, for example." The key is ensuring that the data is secure and that there is a secure point of access. "That adds another dimension to work at home in the financial world that isn't seen as much in other places," he admits, but adds, "It can be done; it's just a matter, from a technical perspective, of watching your Ps and Qs."

4.1 Office equipment and tools

Generally speaking, an employee working from home will need access to the same tools and equipment that allow him or her to be effective and productive in the office. Consider, for instance, the needs of a technical writer: He or she would need a computer with word processing software. To communicate with those back at the office, he or she would also need a telephone and e-mail capability.

Depending on the type of work involved and the need for conferencing between clients — internal and external — it may also be necessary to consider conference calling and other special options for the telephone service. A fax machine may not be necessary if the employee can send documents via e-mail. Similarly, a photocopier may not be necessary if the telecommuter has administrative support available through the head office. And, of course, the technical writer will need a desk, office chair, filing space, and office supplies.

When considering the equipment necessary to establish a home office, it is important to achieve a balance between nice-to-have items and their impact on resources and productivity. It might be nice for a technical writer working with colleagues in various locations to have access to teleconferencing equipment, but it might not have enough impact on productivity to justify the expense.

When providing equipment for employees, one important consideration is compatibility with the equipment at the office. The employee's computer, for instance, should be powerful enough to accommodate the type of work he or she will be doing. Software programs should be the same type and version as coworkers will be using, and e-mail programs should be compatible with those at the head office.

Who should pay for this equipment? For a number of reasons, it is best if the employer covers the costs. If you own the equipment, you have the right to tell the employee to use that equipment for business only. This can be particularly important if the employee will have access to sensitive company or customer information. Owning the equipment will also allow you to make decisions about the type of hardware, software, and other peripherals the employee should be using, and will ensure that your information-system staff is able to provide support for that equipment.

Even if an employee works from home, the employer should make sure that the employee's home office meets standard safety requirements.

The Smart Valley, Inc.® *Telecommuting Guide* includes a checklist that provides a good starting point for determining what your telecommuters may need — or want — in their home-office environments. It is reproduced here as Checklist 1. You may come up with additional items based on your business needs, especially to ensure that any information shared between your business and the telecommuter is secure.

4.2 Safety considerations

There are a variety of safety issues to be considered when setting up a home office, and, of course, there is the issue of who should take responsiblity for ensuring the safety of the home office.

In November 1999, the Occupational Safety and Health Administration (OSHA) released an ill-fated advisory indicating that employers would be responsible for the safety of employees when working from their homes. The outcry from employers, employees, and citizens was loud and immediate. The letter was withdrawn on January 5, 2000, but the discussions continued. Labor Secretary Alexis M. Herman began conducting a series of meetings with business, labor, and government leaders to review the needs of the growing telecommuting population, intending to issue a new set of guidelines to ensure telecommuters' safety and health. At the time of writing, the matter has not been resolved. But even without specific rules from OSHA or other agencies, the vast majority of organizations that allow employees to telecommute do have safety provisions and requirements for their at-home workers.

The Interagency Telecommuting Program's manual, sponsored jointly by the Federal Department of Transportation and General Services Administration, provides guidelines and a home-safety checklist that home-based workers must submit to their supervisors for approval. The checklist is reproduced here as Checklist 2. The guidelines cover technical hazards as well as ergonomic issues.

CHECKLIST 1
FURNITURE, EQUIPMENT, AND SUPPLIES CHECKLIST

Furniture

- ❑ Desk
- ❑ Chair
- ❑ Filing Cabinet
- ❑ Bookcase
- ❑ Credenza
- ❑ Floor Lamp
- ❑ Side Chair
- ❑ Printer Table
- ❑ Sofa
- ❑ Coffee Table
- ❑ Stereo
- ❑ Pictures
- ❑ Conference Table
- ❑ Cork Board
- ❑ White Board
- ❑ Plants
- ❑ Keyboard Extension

Equipment

- ❑ Copier
- ❑ Fax machine
- ❑ Computer Printer
- ❑ Calculator
- ❑ Stapler
- ❑ 2-line Telephone
- ❑ Cordless Telephone
- ❑ Clock
- ❑ Pencil Sharpener
- ❑ Rolodex File
- ❑ Scanner
- ❑ Answering Machine
- ❑ In/Out Baskets
- ❑ Caller ID Equipment
- ❑ Coffee Pot
- ❑ Television
- ❑ Typewriter
- ❑ VCR
- ❑ Micro Recorder
- ❑ Surge Protector
- ❑ Extension Cords

Supplies

- ❑ Hanging Folders
- ❑ Stationery
- ❑ Tape
- ❑ Pen, Pencils
- ❑ Printer Paper
- ❑ Rubber Bands
- ❑ Paper Clips
- ❑ Large Envelopes
- ❑ Ring Binders
- ❑ Note Pads
- ❑ Dictionary
- ❑ Thesaurus
- ❑ Computer Disks
- ❑ Sticky Notes
- ❑ Ruler
- ❑ Calendar
- ❑ Staple Remover
- ❑ Correction Fluid
- ❑ Mailing Labels
- ❑ Highlighters
- ❑ Felt Tip Markers
- ❑ File Folders
- ❑ Copier Paper
- ❑ Fax Paper
- ❑ Push Pins

CHECKLIST 2
TELECOMMUTING SAFETY CHECKLIST

Self-certification Safety Checklist for Home-based Telecommuters
US Office of Personnel Management (www.opm.gov)

The following checklist is designed to assess the overall safety of your alternative worksite. Please read and complete the self-certification safety checklist. Upon completion, you and your supervisor should sign and date the checklist in the spaces provided.

Name: ______________________________

Organization: ______________________________

Address: ______________________________

City/State: ______________________________

Business Telephone: ______________________________

Telecommuting Coordinator: ______________________________

Alternative Worksite Location: ______________________________

____

____

(Describe the designated work area in the alternative worksite.)

A. Workplace Environment

1. Are temperature, noise, ventilation, and lighting levels adequate for maintaining your normal level of job performance? Yes_____ No_____
2. Are all stairs with four or more steps equipped with handrails? Yes_____ No_____
3. Are all circuit breakers and/or fuses in the electrical panel labeled as to intended service? Yes_____ No_____
4. Do circuit breakers clearly indicate if they are in the open or closed position? Yes_____ No_____

Checklist 2 — Continued

5.	Is all electrical equipment free of recognized hazards that would cause physical harm (frayed wires, bare conductors, loose wires, flexible wires running through walls, exposed wires to the ceiling)?	Yes_____	No_____
6.	Will the building's electrical system permit the grounding of electrical equipment?	Yes_____	No_____
7.	Are aisles, doorways, and corners free of obstructions to permit visibility and movement?	Yes_____	No_____
8.	Are file cabinets and storage closets arranged so drawers and doors do not open into walkways?	Yes_____	No_____
9.	Do chairs have any loose casters (wheels) and are the rungs and legs of the chairs sturdy?	Yes_____	No_____
10.	Are the phone lines, electrical cords, and extension wires secured under a desk or alongside a baseboard?	Yes_____	No_____
11.	Is the office space neat, clean, and free of excessive amounts of combustibles?	Yes_____	No_____
12.	Are floor surfaces clean, dry, level, and free of worn or frayed seams?	Yes_____	No_____
13.	Are carpets well secured to the floor and free of frayed or worn seams?	Yes_____	No_____
14.	Is there enough light for reading?	Yes_____	No_____

B. Computer Workstation (if applicable)

15.	Is your chair adjustable?	Yes_____	No_____
16.	Do you know how to adjust your chair?	Yes_____	No_____
17.	Is your back adequately supported by a backrest?	Yes_____	No_____
18.	Are your feet on the floor or fully supported by a footrest?	Yes_____	No_____
19.	Are you satisfied with the placement of monitor and keyboard?	Yes_____	No_____
20.	Is it easy to read the text on your screen?	Yes_____	No_____
21.	Do you need a document holder?	Yes_____	No_____

Checklist 2 — Continued

22. Do you have enough leg room at your desk? Yes_____ No_____
23. Is the screen free from noticeable glare? Yes_____ No_____
24. Is the top of the screen at eye level? Yes_____ No_____
25. Is there space to rest your arms while not keying? Yes_____ No_____
26. When keying, are your forearms close to parallel with the floor? Yes_____ No_____
27. Are your wrists fairly straight when keying? Yes_____ No_____

______________________________ ______________________________

Employee Signature Date

______________________________ ______________________________

Immediate Supervisor's Signature Date

Approved ❒ Disapproved ❒

Please return a copy of this form to your telecommuting program coordinator.

This checklist was developed by the General Services Administration.

(US Office of Personnel Management, <www.opm.gov>)

AG Communication Systems, a subsidiary of Lucent Technologies, has about 10 percent of its workforce operating as full-time or part-time telecommuters. Their safety guidelines focus more on the personal work habits of employees:

When setting up your computer work station you need to:

Prevent neck and back strain and pain:

- Organize workstation so everything is in comfortable reach
- Allow enough room under desktop to move legs
- Position screen 18–24 inches from face
- Set up screen and document holder just below eye level and close enough together to avoid looking back and forth
- Angle screen so you don't have to strain to read it
- Place keyboard so all the keys are easy to reach
- Use a chair with fairly flat seat and an adjustable backrest that supports the lower back
- Sit with back straight, eyes parallel to the screen
- Shift positions regularly without leaving chair

Prevent eyestrain:

- Place screen to avoid back-light glare
- Use dimmer light than you would for most tasks
- Place lighting so it won't shine in your eyes
- Place the monitor screen at right angles to window to prevent glare
- Use nonreflective monitor screen or screen cover
- Choose indirect lighting where possible to prevent glare
- Shield lights around desk to prevent glare
- Adjust monitor brightness and contrast controls for best picture

- Adjust window blinds or shades to eliminate glare
- Keep monitor screen clean, using glass cleaner or water on lint-free cloth
- Look away from screen for a second or two periodically
- Roll, blink, or close eyes tightly for a few seconds periodically
- Consult an eye doctor if eye strain continues, to determine if new or different glasses or eye exercises are needed

Prevent carpal tunnel syndrome:

- Keep hands, wrists, and forearms straight and parallel to floor while working, with elbows at 90 degree angle
- Take breaks periodically to stretch, shake out hands
- Recognize symptoms immediately

Prevent stress:

- Follow procedures to reduce neck and back pain and eyestrain
- Don't rush
- Don't become angry or frustrated with a customer

One or both of these approaches to developing safety standards for telecommuting employees should help you decide what will work best for your business.

Do the events surrounding the Occupational Health and Safety Administration's issuance — and later retraction — of a document outlining employer responsibility for employee safety outside the brick-and-mortar workplace mean that you should reconsider any telecommuting activities?

No. Telecommuting will continue. Employees will continue to take work home with them from time to time. And in the process of doing that work, some employees will be injured. Might you be responsible for those injuries? Yes.

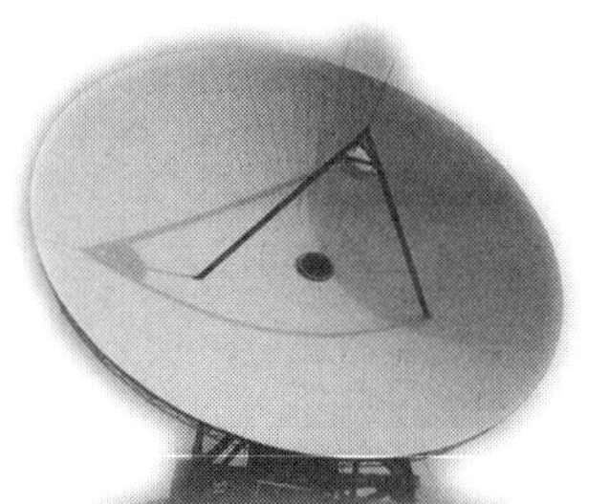

There are many good reasons to implement a telecommuting program, including cost savings, increased productivity, and increased employee recruitment and retention.

Employers need to be responsible for employee safety. The problem is that in an era of virtual work, the bounds of that responsibility are very unclear. If an employee is injured due to an electrical shock because of a frayed cord on the computer in his or her home office, which was supplied by the employer, is the employer at fault? Most reasonable adults would say, "Probably." But is the employer at fault if that same employee slipped and fell on the way to the bathroom while working at home? Most reasonable adults would say, "Probably not."

There are obviously no easy answers. The boundaries between work and home are becoming increasingly blurred. The solution is to develop very clear policies and guidelines regarding safety issues of employees working from home.

5. The Characteristics of a Successful Program

Telecommuting can and does work in companies large and small, located in both rural and urban locations. But success depends on careful planning and well-established guidelines, as well as appropriate selection of both the positions and the people who will participate in telecommuting.

You should institute a telecommuting program for the right reasons. You should not institute a telecommuting program simply because an employee has requested the option or because it seems to be a current trend. Like any other business decision you make, the decision to allow employees to telecommute should be based on legitimate and demonstrable business benefits.

The details of implementing a telecommuting program will vary from business to business, depending on the particular needs of the organization. Yet there are many needs and concerns that span the spectrum of the business world, and familiarity with the techniques of other organizations will get you thinking about what will work for you. Sample 1 provides ideas for how to make your program a success.

6. Case Study

In May of 1997, Jennifer Johnson had recently been promoted to a marketing executive position at Novell in Utah. She was heading out for a three-day trip to New York City, Minneapolis, and San Francisco

SAMPLE 1
PRESCRIPTION FOR IMPLEMENTING TELEWORK

Jim Miller (a.k.a. Dr. Telework), general manager of US West Extended Workplace solutions, shares the following prescription for implementing telework:

(a) **Identify how telework fits with your company's goals.** Know why you want to implement telework at your company, and set goals accordingly. Do you want to increase productivity? Cut down on wasted travel time? Retain valuable employees? If you don't have a clear sense of what you want to achieve through telework, you'll never achieve it.

(b) **Determine which jobs are eligible for telework.** Telework is not for everyone. Know why you want your employees to work at home and determine which ones are the best candidates. Make sure your reasons are realistic — and truly beneficial to both the company and employee.

(c) **Sell the benefits.** Once you understand the benefits of telework, sell them to the other people involved. Talk to your employees about the personal benefits to them. If there's no benefit to them, why should they buy in?

(d) **Avoid surprises and anticipate problems.** Plan ahead. Personnel policies, communication, and technology issues need to be assessed prior to adopting telework. What part of your employees' jobs will be made more difficult by teleworking? How will you overcome these obstacles? Know the answers before you implement telework.

(e) **Build a good work environment at home.** Make sure your employees have a work environment at home that's conducive to work. That usually means having a room devoted solely to work. The home work environment must be equal to or better than the office environment from a safety and ergonomics perspective.

(f) **Have the right telework tools.** Technology can be a critical time saver or a literal time hog. Whether it is high-speed data transfer lines or a 300Mhz Pentium II processor, the technology at home must match the tasks to be performed.

(g) **Maintain strong personal connections.** How do your employees maintain their communications link with coworkers and managers in the office? How do they fit in the office hierarchy and compete for promotions? How will you make your teleworkers feel connected and appreciated?

(h) **Train for telework.** Telework is different than working in an office. Provide training to help your employees succeed in their new environment. Don't give your employees a computer, a pager, and a phone line and expect them to be successful teleworkers. That goes double for managers back at the office. They need training on how to manage remotely and how to manage by results.

(i) **Evaluate your telework activity.** If you're just starting out on the telework journey, keep tabs on how it's going at points along the way. Review your progress against your telework goals (see first tip) and make any mid-course corrections.

(j) **Remember, we're all human.** Take into account the human needs of your employees. Just because they're not in the office every day doesn't mean they don't need to socialize with coworkers.

Virtual agency Johnson & Company has a Web site, rather than an office building, as its corporate headquarters.

for a series of focus groups that were part of a new product introduction her business unit was involved in. Her schedule was tight and involved meeting up with her husband, who was also traveling, so that he could take their small child. "I looked like I was one of the Clampetts, wheeling through the airport with one of those smart carts with luggage and a child strategically placed," she says. "We got to the gate and found out my husband's flight was ten minutes late. I had to wait, agonizingly, until he got there and then I had to race to my terminal." She made her flight but says, "I decided that, for me, the corporate, high-stress travel thing wasn't going to cut it."

While at Novell, Johnson had developed an infrastructure of marketing people she could call upon for assistance outside the traditional agency relationship. She had been working with a marketing agency that was assigned to her business unit and found that "they were not interested in learning our business." She began to wonder if there weren't other marketing executives at other organizations that were facing the same frustrations and that had the same need for "a core of really talented, motivated, experienced people." She began to recruit a team of people — all women — who had dropped out of the workforce, and she asked them to come together to form a virtual company.

In June 1997, she incorporated the virtual agency she had developed as Johnson & Company. In May 1998, she struck out on her own, giving up the stability — and the high stress — of her position at Novell. "It wasn't until the demand for work exceeded my resources that I realized that I could start to leverage this infrastructure I had put in place," she says.

Today, Johnson's virtual agency operates with 15 associates who work in four different time zones, all out of their homes. "We say that our corporate headquarters is www.joandco.com," she says, "and it really is." Johnson & Company operates like any Madison Avenue public relations and ad agency. The firm targets companies that are going public — many of which are dot com companies. "We believe in working any time, any place, any way, and at any pace," Johnson says. "We use that as our guide in figuring out how to operate as a virtual business."

Recruiting has occurred primarily through word of mouth and referrals ("A lot of our associates are former Novell alums," Johnson says). Contacts are also made through trade shows and conferences.

Managing telecommuters isn't really much different from managing traditional employees, Johnson says. "A lot of the issues are the same as you have with managing in general, but with an added level of complexity. The issue I would point to is one of organization. You really need to have a plan and you need to understand different people's work hours. We work with multiple time zones so there's a lot of math that needs to go on with any project!"

The underlying component of managing telecommuters, Johnson stresses, is trust. "You have to trust that they're honest and they're capable at what they're doing." Communication is also critical. "Managers need to understand that they need to be the very best examples in terms of keeping telecommuters in the loop for information and in terms of treating them the same as their 'brick-and-mortar' colleagues."

She points to both a cultural and a technical aspect of managing telecommuters. The cultural side involves trust and communication. The technical side involves the appropriate tools to allow telecommuters to function effectively. "You need to find tools that help to remove the barriers of time and place."

Johnson points out that there are many corporations that have already successfully figured out how to manage telecommuting — they just may not think of what they're doing in those terms. "Anyone who has worked in a global company and has been involved as part of a team is already familiar with these concepts," she says. At Novell, Johnson managed the marketing efforts for Asia-Pacific and European offices. "I would host calls at midnight my time to accommodate the different time zones," she says. "We were really doing a lot of the same things that I'm trying to do with Johnson & Company now."

Her message for any company is "You can do any idea you want from anywhere you want with the available technology and the new attitudes people have about collaboration. Telework is really a great liberator if we can get creative on how to make it happen."

Chapter 3
POLICIES AND PROCEDURES

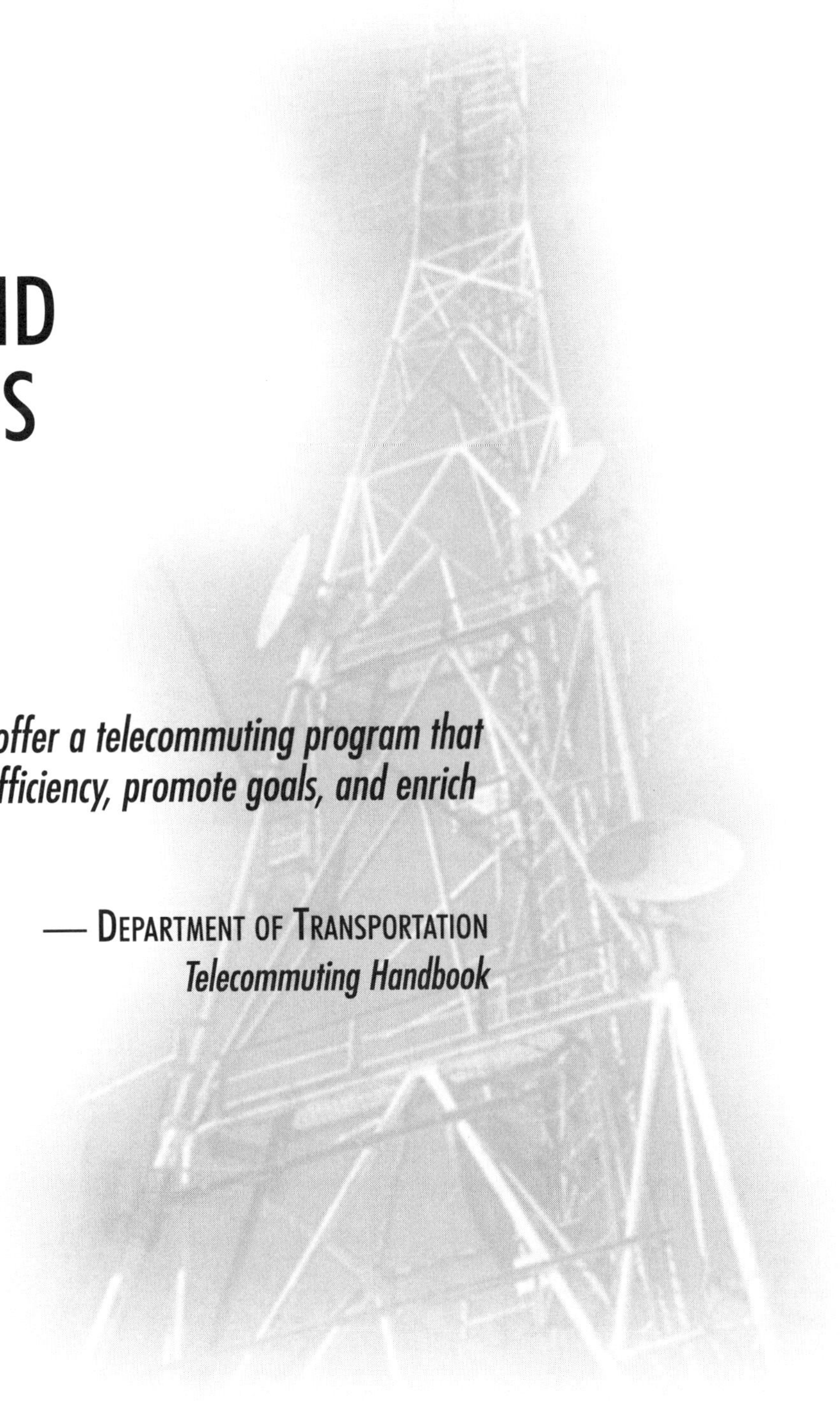

"It is (company) policy to offer a telecommuting program that will enhance operational efficiency, promote goals, and enrich the quality of work life."

— DEPARTMENT OF TRANSPORTATION
Telecommuting Handbook

Executive Summary

What can I do to control overtime expenses among my telecommuters?

Hourly or nonexempt employees need to be compensated for hours they work in excess of 40 hours in a work week. This means telecommuters as well. One way of addressing this issue with hourly staff, not unlike dealing with the issue of overtime with traditional staff, is to clearly communicate to telecommuters that they are expected to work no more than their scheduled time. Any overtime must be pre-approved by the employee's manager, and accurate records of hours worked must be kept.

Could I be charged with discrimination based on a decision to let a certain employee telecommute and not another?

Employers may not discriminate in making decisions related to employees based on their race, gender, national origin, age, religion, or with respect to certain disabilities. The need to treat employees equitably also applies to telecommuters and is an important reason why the decision to allow an employee to telecommute must be based on objective criteria. Decisions should not be based solely on the employee's personal/family needs, and employers should never show favoritism toward certain individuals.

Can I be required to allow a disabled employee to telecommute?

The Americans with Disabilities Act (ADA) requires employers to make "reasonable accommodations" for employees with physical or mental disabilities. In some cases, telecommuting can offer a reasonable accommodation, meeting the needs of both the organization and the disabled worker. While it is likely that courts could require companies that have telecommuting programs to offer telecommuting as an option to disabled workers, it is not likely that courts would require this same accommodation from companies that do not otherwise offer telecommuting as an option.

If a telecommuter gets injured at home, is he or she eligible for Workers' Compensation?

Telecommuting employees are eligible for workers' compensation benefits if injured during the "course and scope of employment." The issue of whether, and to what extent, employers are liable for the safety of their employees when they are working out of their homes has been the source of much discussion recently. As an employer, you should establish standards for safety and require employees to follow those standards.

Should I require access to my telecommuter's home office?

The ability to visit an employee at his or her home location should be an issue that is addressed in your telecommuting policy. Visits should be made for business purposes only and should be announced in advance. Issues of employee privacy and company liability surface here, as does concern over potential claims of inappropriate behavior between the visitor and the employee. Can you, as a manager, go to an employee's home to check up on him or her? Yes, but you may not want to. If you do, make sure that you reserve this right and establish some guidelines related to the hours you may visit and the length of notice you should provide.

POLICIES AND PROCEDURES

There are myriad details to consider when establishing a telecommuting program. It can be the little things that often create the most frustration and require the most effort — things like coming up with an appropriate contract for the program, or dealing with performance measurement, or figuring out how to deal with certain legal issues that affect the employee/employer relationship. This chapter discusses the kinds of policies and procedures that you will have to implement in your business to make telecommuting work for you. See the Appendixes for sample policies, agreements, and guidelines that have made telecommuting a success for other organizations.

1. Policy Considerations

The more specific and clear you can be about the requirements and processes for your telecommuting program, the fewer misunderstandings or problems you will encounter. Considering policy and procedure issues *before* you receive requests from employees who wish to telecommute will help you make good decisions based upon the needs of your organization.

There are a number of policy issues you will want to consider, many of which are listed below.

1.1 Work hours

One of the benefits the telecommuting employee receives is flexibility in hours of work. But that flexibility must still be tied to the needs of the workplace — including the needs of coworkers and customers (internal and external). Being available to take phone calls or respond to e-mail messages may be critical for some telecommuting positions, but not to others. For example, an employee working in a virtual call center operation and answering calls at home would need to be available to take calls from customers at specific, established times throughout the day. A computer programmer working at home, however, may not have the same access requirements. Each position will vary, but for each position, you should very clearly indicate the hours you expect the employee to be working.

There are a variety of work-hour options for telecommuters, as indicated in the chart below from AGCS entitled "Teleworker Category Matrix." Note that teleworker type is used to determine hardware and software needs as well as meeting frequency.

1.2 Work assignments

How will work assignments be provided? Will the employee be required to meet or contact the supervisor on a regularly scheduled basis to discuss assignments, or will assignments be made as they occur? What will the assignments consist of?

1.3 Evaluation

How will the employee's work be evaluated? What level of productivity will be expected? What are the criteria by which the employee's work output will be judged? Be specific. By clearly outlining expectations at the outset, you can avoid misunderstanding and frustration later.

1.4 Salary and benefits

What will the employee's pay be? Will the employee be hourly or salaried? What benefits will apply? Chances are, your criteria for pay and benefits for telecommuters will be the same as those for other employees. Even if this is the case, be sure to clearly spell out these terms so both you and the telecommuter know what to expect.

Teleworker Category Matrix

Type of Teleworker	Casual	Part-Time	Job Demand	Full-Time	Mobile
Frequency of Teleworking	Occasionally takes work home or may be in addition to the normal work day	Works at home on a schedule — 1 or more days per week	Required by job to work 8 or more non-prime hours per week at home	Works primarily from home	Has the need to conduct business from a number of locations, is a frequent traveler
Hardware	Personally owned system. Modem from ITS.	Personally owned system. Communication device from ITS.	AGCS-owned desktop system	AGCS-owned desktop system	Assigned a laptop or checks one out from a shared pool
Software	Selected software from ITS, installed via disk.	Selected software from ITS, installed via disk	ITS installed	ITS installed	ITS installed
Communication Support	Dial-in	Data line, if available. Set up/monthly charges paid by AGCS.	Data line, if available. Set up/monthly charges paid by AGCS.	Data line, if available. Set up/monthly charges paid by AGCS.	Dial-in
Primary Office Location	AGCS facility	AGCS facility	AGCS facility	Home. May reserve shared space (hoteling).	Varies
Meeting Attendance	In person	In person or via telephone	In person	Primarily via telephone	Yes, as available

(© 1996 AG Communication Systems)

1.5 Overtime

One of the concerns that many employers have about allowing employees to work from home is that they cannot be monitored. The potential exists for more time to be devoted to a project than might be necessary. One way to address this concern, particularly with hourly employees, is to have a policy that overtime will be not allowed unless approved by the supervisor. Another is to establish clear expectations about productivity. This is, of course, easier to do when you have a number of employees whose work output can be compared.

1.6 Equipment

Will the employer provide equipment for the employee? Will the employee be allowed to use his or her own equipment? If the employee can use his or her own equipment, will he or she be compensated for that use? Will repairs to employee-owned equipment be paid by the employer? Be specific in outlining your equipment policies, addressing issues such as confidentiality, personal use, upgrades, and return of equipment upon termination.

2. Documenting Your Policies and Procedures

Whether outlined in your telecommuting policy, contract, or agreement, you should provide specific written documentation of the understanding between you and your telecommuters. This document should cover all of the details that will determine how the telecommuting arrangement works, how the telecommuter will interact with the head office, and what the company's expectations are for the relationship.

2.1 Policy statement

Your policy statement should include general discussion about the telecommuting policy of your company, indicating the applications of the program and its goals. The Department of Transportation *Telecommuting Handbook* (www.tasc.dot.gov) provides the following sample:

> It is (company) policy to offer a telecommuting program that will enhance operational efficiency, promote program goals, and enrich the

> quality of work life. This program enhances an employee's ability to meet both his or her professional and personal responsibilities. At the same time, the responsible officials must ensure that telecommuting achieves such goals as increased operational efficiency, reduced operating costs, increased service to the public, and improved recruitment and retention of employees.

The policy statement should also include information about participation in the program. The Department of Transportation *Telecommuting Handbook* states:

> Participation in the telecommuting program is voluntary. Supervisors are responsible for determining which positions are appropriate for telecommuting and for making decisions on employee requests to participate. The supervisor must consider the employee's performance level, ability to handle responsibility, and self-motivation on an individual basis.

You may wish to specify the supervisor's role in determining the details of the telecommuting arrangement. For example, you might discuss the supervisor's right to determine the length, duration, and time frames of the arrangement (i.e., how many days per week are appropriate); and/or the supervisor's evaluation schedule and the criteria by which the telecommuter's performance will be judged.

You may also wish to address specific requirements of the program, such as —

- requiring a signed telecommuting work agreement for all participants, and/or
- requiring training as a prerequisite to telecommuting.

You might consider including in your policy statement some discussion of what is *not* acceptable in a telecommuting program. For example, you might state that working from home is not an alternative to dependant care.

See Appendix 2 for a sample policy.

2.2 Selection criteria

Specific selection criteria will help you avoid discrimination charges arising out of claims of favoritism. Criteria may include such traits as self-motivation, strong communication skills, and the ability to work independently. In addition, selection criteria should include factors related to the types of jobs or tasks that can be performed off-site. The more specific you are as to what criteria are acceptable, the more smoothly your program will run.

The Department of Transportation *Telecommuting Handbook* states:

> Participants should be employed by (company) for more than 90 days, though special situations could occur that would permit a new employee to telecommute, particularly special need individuals. Employees in a temporary, trainee, or probationary position would not be eligible to telecommute, as these employees usually need close supervision and frequent interaction with supervisors or mentors.

2.3 Expectations/responsibilities of telecommuters

The contract should outline the expectations that the company has of its telecommuting staff, detailing as much as possible, from furnishings to security issues. The Department of Transportation provides a condensed summary of expectations in its *Telecommuting Handbook:*

> All telecommuters will be required to sign and abide by a written letter of agreement, participate in mandatory evaluations, and, for home work situations, provide an adequate home work station that ensures privacy and a lack of interruptions. Telecommuters must be responsible for the security of all official data, protection of government furnished equipment and property, and carrying out the mission of (the company) in an alternate work setting. Performance will be evaluated on finished assignments under a management by results approach. Participating in the Telecommuting Program is offered only with the agreement that it is the employee's responsibility to provide a proper work environment.

2.4 Work schedules

The requirements of each individual position will determine the hours in which the work needs to take place. Certain positions (in-bound telephone sales reps, for instance) may be required to be available during certain hours of the day, while others (computer programmers, for example) may not have such restrictions. The Department of Transportation *Telecommuting Handbook* provides a very good example of how to approach this issue:

> Work schedules will vary according to the individual arrangement between employee and supervisor. All schedules will be agreed upon, in advance, and should be on a fixed schedule. . . . All regulations regarding absence and leave apply to telecommuters. Supervisors must approve work schedules, in advance, to ensure the employee's time and attendance records are properly certified and to preclude any liability for premium or overtime pay, unless specifically approved, in advance. Compensatory time may be granted in lieu of overtime pay in accordance with applicable regulations. Periodic adjustment to the work schedule is desirable to achieve the best mix of organizational requirements and employee performance.

2.5 Equipment and supplies

This section of the agreement should outline, in detail, the equipment and supplies that will be provided by the company and those that will be the responsibility of the telecommuter. Standards, where applicable, should also be included (i.e., requirements for certain types of furniture based on safety considerations, etc.). Indicate, also, whether and to what extent the telecommuter will be responsible for maintenance and repair of equipment, what the employer's role will be, and how repairs will be handled (i.e., equipment will need to be brought into the office or the company will send a repair person to the employee's home location). Again, be as specific as possible to avoid any employee confusion or dissatisfaction. The Department of Transportation *Telecommuting Handbook* discusses this matter in detail:

> Supervisors may authorize use of computers and other telecommunications equipment in a home office, provided the equipment is used only for official business and requested equipment is available for use in a home office. Participation in a telecommuting agreement may be contingent on the availability of equipment or the availability of funds to purchase equipment needed to perform the official duties. Each arrangement must be examined on a case-by-case basis before final approval in order to make decisions on the type of equipment needed and its availability.

The employee must protect all equipment from possible theft and environmental damage. In cases of damage to unsecured equipment by non-employees, the employee may be held liable for repair or replacement of the equipment, software, etc., in compliance with applicable regulations on negligence. The employee must notify the supervisor immediately following a malfunction of (company-owned) equipment. If repairs are extensive, the employee may be asked to report to the traditional office until repairs are completed.

2.6 Insurance

You should verify what type of coverage is afforded the telecommuter based upon your existing insurance policy, and decide whether the employee will be responsible for providing any additional coverage. The employee should indemnify the company from any injuries claimed by any third parties and should be required to maintain appropriate insurance coverage for these types of claims.

2.7 Employer's right to inspect workplace

Clearly indicate if and when the company or manager will have the right to inspect or visit the employee's off-site work location. For instance, you may want to reserve the right to access the home office for purposes of safety inspections, accident investigations, equipment audits, or other business-related matters. Visits are usually based upon reasonable notice — generally 24 hours, or less, if agreed to by the employee.

2.8 Privacy and confidentiality

Employees working from their homes, particularly those who are connected to the home office electronically, present a certain amount of security risk for your organization. Consider having telecommuters sign confidentiality agreements and indicate in your agreement whether or not the telecommuter may use computer equipment for non-work-related activities. Security procedures must be discussed in detail, with emphasis upon the need for strict adherence to the procedures.

2.9 Performance measurement

The telecommuting employee and his or her manager should work together to come up with applicable quantitative measures of performance. These measures should be documented as part of the telecommuting agreement and should clearly indicate what the expectations are of the employee in terms of quantity and quality of work, as well as how often and in what manner the telecommuting employee's performance will be measured.

2.10 Company policies

Include a statement in your telecommuting document to indicate that telecommuters will be required to abide by all existing company policies and procedures, except as they differ from specific items as outlined in the telecommuting agreement.

2.11 Termination of the agreement

Your telecommuting agreement should include a section dealing with the potential termination of the agreement by either the company or manager, or the telecommuter. It should detail the situation(s) under which the agreement might be terminated (i.e., inability to perform work duties as outlined in the agreement). It should also discuss the employee's options upon termination of the agreement — can the employee maintain the position in-house, or can he or she apply for another in-house position, or is the employee terminated from the company? The termination agreement must also address the disposition of any company equipment that has been purchased for the employee's use at home.

2.12 Employment-at-will disclaimer

The telecommuting agreement does not constitute a contract of employment. The agreement should indicate that the telecommuting employee remains employed on an at-will basis and can be terminated with or without cause and with or without notice.

3. Case Study

Carolyn Lamothe is a project officer for Industry Canada in the Information Highway Applications Branch for SchoolNet. She is one of 258 employees in the branch, and she is a telecommuter. Telecommuting has been an option for about four years.

Lamothe telecommutes three days a week, typically going into the office on Tuesdays and Thursdays to meet with coworkers "to obtain updates and work out any problems that may arise." She decided to try telecommuting because "I had a lot of projects on the go at the same time with short time frames and a lot of work to accomplish in a small amount of time." Her commute was 45 minutes each way and, she says, "I had the stress at work, along with my family; I was trying to be the perfect woman." It was too much. "So, I decided to try telework."

She approached her manager about the option of working from home and was surprised and elated when her manager agreed to let her try. At the beginning, she says, "I was thrilled. I could work from home and still please my family." Then the problems began.

"Because I was working from home, I could be accessible day or night," she recalls. "I started receiving phone calls from clients all over the country during supper time with the family. Of course my family was upset because this wasn't supposed to happen anymore." Fortunately, she learned to manage the interruptions by getting a cell phone and using a voice-mail message indicating the hours of the day when she was available. Now, she says, "Everything is working smoothly."

"Teleworking is wonderful," Lamothe says, but adds, "From time to time you do feel lonely." She uses a variety of means to stay in touch with the office, including e-mail, telephone, and personal meetings. "I feel communications is the key," she says. "As long as you keep your manager up to date on everything that is happening with respect to your workload, then everything should work out."

She suggests to managers that with just as when supervising traditional employees, a little recognition can go a long way with telecommuters. "Send them an e-mail from time to time to let them know you appreciate the work they are doing."

Chapter 4
HIRING EXISTING STAFF AS TELECOMMUTERS

"[Telecommuting] is not a right, it's a management alternative."

— ALAN COLEMAN
of Sprint

Executive Summary

What if all of my employees decide they want to telecommute?

It's unlikely that all of your employees will decide that telecommuting is right for them. In fact, many employees prefer to work in the traditional setting. Remember, whether telecommuting is appropriate for an individual or a position is a decision that must be made by the manager and the organization.

Is telecommuting appropriate for hourly workers?

In general, yes. However, you will want to check the employment law statutes in your area to make sure there are no laws that prohibit non-exempt employees from working as telecommuters.

Can managers be telecommuters?

Yes! In fact, many managers do operate, in effect, as telecommuting managers when they are responsible for supervising employees who may be located in other offices — even in other countries!

What are the characteristics of a successful telecommuter?

Good employees make good telecommuters — they are independent thinkers, self-starters, and productive workers who clearly understand the requirements of the job and can work effectively with little or no supervision.

How do I deal with employees who are not able to telecommute?

Telecommuting should be explained to employees as a job variation rather than a benefit. Your telecommuting policy should clearly indicate the types of positions and personal qualifications that are required for telecommuters. Beyond this, there may be other flexible work options that employees not right for telecommuting can take advantage of.

Does an employee have the right to telecommute?

No. The decision on whether or not to allow an employee to telecommute should be made by the employer based on the appropriateness of both the position and the employee's skills and capabilities. This decision should be based upon specific criteria that are applied to all potential telecommuting candidates.

HIRING EXISTING STAFF AS TELECOMMUTERS

Now that you have a good idea of what telecommuting is all about and you know how to create an effective telecommuting policy for your business, it is time to think about the people who will ultimately make the program a success. It is time to think about your telecommuters!

In the vast majority of situations, telecommuters come from within the organization and have held a position with the company for some time before making the transition to telecommuter. There are obvious benefits to selecting telecommuters from your existing staff. You already know these people! You've had a chance to view their work habits and performance. You know which of your employees are independent and proactive and which employees need constant supervision and direction.

But there can be downfalls as well, particularly if you don't take the time to make informed and carefully considered choices about which employees are offered the opportunity to telecommute.

Just as you need a system for creating policies and procedures for your telecommuting program, so too do you need a systematic approach to considering individual telecommuting candidates. How structured your selection criteria are will depend on your company's culture as well as on your comfort level with the concept of telecommuting. Even companies that have been committed to telecommuting for some time often have very stringent criteria for selecting telecommuting candidates.

A well-developed, formal selection process helps organizations to avoid possible pitfalls.

Alan Coleman of Sprint, a company that has been practicing telecommuting for years — "since modems were created," Coleman says — has established what he refers to as "a fairly laborious process to become a telecommuter." Sprint has 650 full-time telecommuters with more than 20,000 employees telecommuting informally, according to Coleman.

The process was formalized, he says, for a number of reasons:

(a) To ensure that people wouldn't begin pouring home in massive numbers

(b) To make sure that management had adequate knowledge of the job functions that were being performed at home

(c) To allow executives to see how business units were actually managing their individual units

(d) To allow for accurate evaluation of the success, failure, and costs of telecommuting to the company.

At Sprint, the managers drive the process of telecommuting. That's not to say that individual employees can't request that their position be considered for telecommuting. It simply means that the manager is in charge and is expected to make an appropriate determination of whether telecommuting is or is not appropriate for his or her particular work unit — and a particular employee.

1. Telecommuting Is Not for Everyone

Just as some jobs are more appropriate for telecommuting than others, certain employees are more suited to telecommuting than other employees. Some employees may not even be interested in telecommuting. You may be surprised to find, in fact, that a number of your staff actually prefer the camaraderie and sense of team that the workplace holds. Other employees may simply realize that they are not self-motivated enough to be productive away from the office. Still others have home situations that might make it inconvenient or untenable for them to work there. And many people will find it difficult to maintain a division between home-life and work-life when home and work share a location.

2. Selection Criteria

Some of the criteria for selecting employees who will be good telecommuters are admittedly subjective. Susan Thomas, who leads a telecommuting program for CIGNA, an employee benefits company, says, "We're looking for people who are independent workers, meaning they're comfortable with working alone physically, they're self-motivated, they are good communicators in terms of letting people know where they are, asking questions when questions need to be asked, and seeking out resources." CIGNA has had a formal corporate policy on telecommuting since 1991 and had at least 1,000 active telecommuters in 2000 — many who are responsible for claims processing, but also professional workers including nursing staff and training professionals. Typically, employees work for the company prior to becoming telecommuters, but some positions — in the virtual sales offices, for instance — hire people as telecommuters.

In addition to the soft skills, CIGNA also looks at some quantifiable characteristics. Most telecommuters are required to have six months of service with the company; they must also perform at a level that meets standards, and they must be proficient with a computer.

Successful telecommuters—

- *Stay connected with coworkers and the boss.* This requires a certain amount of proactive communication. Rather than waiting for the phone to ring or for the e-mail message to arrive, successful telecommuters take the initiative to stay connected.
- *Are well organized.* Many telecommuters come from environments in which they had ready access to administrative staff. When working alone, that access may be limited — or nonexistent.
- *Get out of the house.* Telecommuting doesn't mean hibernating. Successful telecommuters take advantage of opportunities to network with coworkers, peers, and other colleagues by making lunch dates, being active in professional associations, and generally staying in touch.

- *Separate home from work.* When working from home it can be difficult to avoid the lure of personal tasks — like washing clothes or taking care of children and pets. It's important to learn how to establish clear boundaries between home and work.
- *Make technology their friend.* Technology has made telecommuting possible and popular. The many tools like e-mail, group scheduling, and teleconferencing make it easy to stay connected, regardless of physical and geographic barriers.
- *Know when to take a break.* A common downfall of telecommuting, according to those who have experienced it, is the tendency to work too much.

Certain employees may prove to be ill-suited to telecommuting. They may include—

- employees who have a high need for social interaction,
- employees who are easily distracted by outside demands and interruptions,
- employees who need the office setting to provide an environment conducive to work, and
- employees who do not have adequate child-care arrangements or supportive family situations.

Telecommuting is not an option that should be available to all employees. Your decision on whether or not to allow an employee to telecommute will depend upon the demands and characteristics of the job as well as the personal traits of the employee. Selection criteria should be carefully considered and clearly outlined in your telecommuting policy and contract.

3. Assessing Telework Candidates

How can you determine whether telework candidates will be suited to this type of work? Your own observation of their performance during their employment with your company can certainly provide some indications. In addition, you will want to spend some time speaking with the employee and exploring the pros and cons of telecommuting to provide both of you with a sense of whether or not this option will be appropriate.

At Merrill Lynch, Pierce, Fenner & Smith, Inc., employees and their managers work jointly to develop a telecommuting arrangement that will work. According to Janice Miholics, vice president, manager of private client technology for alternative work arrangements for Merrill Lynch, the first step for employees interested in telecommuting is to submit a telecommuting proposal. The proposal outlines the days of the week — and even hours of the day — during which the employee would like to telecommute. In addition, the employee is asked to include information on why he or she would be a good candidate for telecommuting, what the benefits are to the employee, to the manager, and to their clients. It is then up to the manager to review the proposal and approve or deny the request. Janice's group reviews all proposals, both approved and denied. This provides a good checkpoint, allowing, for instance, the opportunity to review any rejections and ensure that there are no underlying employee-relations issues. Managers are also expected to document reasons that a candidate was not selected and to spend time with the employee to indicate what the employee may need to do in order to be considered at some future date.

Using an assessment tool in the selection of telecommuting candidates is an effective way to avoid any charges of arbitrariness. Such a tool can provide both the employee and his or her manager with an indication of readiness or appropriateness for telecommuting.

ALLearnatives®, a company in Wexford, Pennsylvania, that provides learning resources and consulting services to individuals and organizations involved in telecommuting, offers the following self-assessment for those interested in telecommuting. This tool can serve as a good starting point in discussions between managers and employees on their readiness or suitability for a telecommuting position.

True	False	I believe I:
		Enjoy working independently.
		Like to think through and resolve problems myself.
		Am a high-initiative person.
		Am not a procrastinator.
		Can set and stick to a schedule.

True	False	I believe I:
		Like to organize and plan.
		Am a self-disciplined person.
		Am able and willing to handle administrative tasks.
		Can balance attention to major objectives and small details.
		Do not need constant interaction with people.
		Can work effectively with little or no feedback from others.
		Enjoy being in my own home.
		Do not need frequent feedback or coaching.
		Have the required level of verbal and written communication skills.
		Can pace myself to avoid both overworking and wasting time.
		Can resist a refrigerator that is only a few steps away.
		JOB APPROPRIATENESS
		My job:
		Requires minimal face-to-face interaction.
		Involves many responsibilities that can be met by phone, fax, or modem.
		Accountabilities can be quantified, measured, and monitored.
		Affords me the freedom to manage my work as I see best.
		Does not require frequent interaction with work associates.
		Involves coworkers who are supportive and collaborative.

True	False	I believe I:
		HOME OFFICE SPACE/EQUIPMENT
		I have a space in my home office that:
		Has an adequate amount of work space for my current needs.
		Would provide opportunities for future expansion.
		Has an adequate amount of storage space.
		Has adequate lighting.
		Has sufficient ventilation.
		Has a safe number of electrical circuits.
		Is quiet enough to allow me to concentrate.
		Provides appropriate separation from home/family distractions.
		Is a pleasant and comfortable space I'd enjoy working in.
		Is a reasonable distance from needed business services.
		Has no zoning or lease restrictions that preclude telecommuting.
		Has adequate insurance coverage to protect business equipment.
		FAMILY SUPPORT
		My family:
		Is supportive of my desire to telecommute and will react positively.
		Is willing to minimize distractions and interruptions.
		Will not require care or involvement from me during work hours.
		Can accept my need to focus on work during business hours.
		Is stable and has no relationship conflicts that would be distracting.

(Reprinted with permission from 101 Tips for Telecommuters *by Debra A. Dinnocenzo. Copyright©1999 by Debra A. Dinnocenzo.)*

When reviewing the form with potential telecommuting candidates, give special consideration to those items that the potential telecommuter has marked as "false." These are the areas that represent potential barriers to success.

Note that the criteria go beyond personal characteristics like "enjoy working independently" to take into account considerations related to the job itself, the home-office environment, and even the family. Each of these characteristics can have an impact on the telecommuter's success, and each needs to be carefully considered.

4. Traits of Successful Teleworkers

A successful employee is a successful employee, whether he or she works from home or at the head office. Assuming that the job is appropriate for the move to telecommuting, you probably already have a good idea of how your telecommuting employee will perform. Yet there are some specific skills that require particular emphasis in a telecommuting position.

Sample 2 is a useful summary of the traits found to be common among successful telecommuters, drawn from the ALLearnatives® assessment tool.

Alongside these core requirements, you will want to look for other qualifications that will make the transition to telecommuting that much more smooth for your employees and, ultimately, for your business. The University of Michigan, for example, includes additonal recommended qualifications in its telecommuting guidelines, as shown in Sample 3.

5. Perils and Pitfalls

Your company and your management staff should be aware of some common issues that may arise when selecting telecommuters internally.

5.1 It just doesn't work

One of the greatest potential pitfalls involved in selecting employees as telecommuters is choosing the wrong employee. Fortunately, it's a pitfall that can be overcome. Not all telecommuters are going to thrive in their new role, regardless of how careful the selection process was, how

SAMPLE 2
COMMON TRAITS OF SUCCESSFUL TELECOMMUTERS

ALLearnatives

Enjoy working independently. An employee who is able to tackle assignments without a great deal of intervention from his or her manager and who feels comfortable working alone, without frequent interaction with coworkers, would be more comfortable working as a telecommuter than an employee who thrives in a team environment.

Like to think through and resolve problems on their own. An employee who asks frequent questions and needs constant reassurance about his or her progress may have a difficult time working in an unsupervised environment. At a minimum, this employee would need to have some well-established communication channels available to maintain ties to the workplace.

Demonstrate high initiative. Employees who thrive in telecommuting settings have demonstrated their independence through a high level of initiative on the job. They are the employees who don't wait to be told what to do next — they generate ideas, tackle assignments, and are able to remain productive with little outside reinforcement.

Do not procrastinate. Production is the name of the game in any employee/employer relationship, and telecommuting is certainly no exception. The issue of procrastination goes directly to many managers' concerns about the "out of sight, out of mind" conundrum. Employees who consistently meet deadlines (without having to frantically pull things together at the last minute) will be best suited for telecommuting. Employees who frequently fail to get assignments completed on time and need a great deal of prompting to move forward would probably not be good telecommuting candidates.

Can set and stick to a schedule. Since employees working from their homes are not directly observed or managed, they need to be comfortable and adept at setting and sticking to their own work schedules. Many organizations require that employees indicate specific times that they will be "working," and this is a good practice. Yet, beyond this, telecommuters must also be able to push themselves to be productive when they're away from the formal drivers that they've been used to.

Are able and willing to handle administrative tasks. In the workplace telecommuters may have been able to take advantage of administrative help that may not be available (or may not be as readily available) once they are telecommuting. Will the telecommuter feel comfortable doing his or her own administrative tasks — filing, making photocopies, etc.?

Do not need constant interaction. This can be a difficult point to assess. Even the most gregarious person may feel perfectly at ease working from home. It's an issue that only the individual can truly address. To help in this assessment, you may want to consider the use of a personality inventory such as the Myers-Briggs assessment.

Have the required level of communication skills. Communication is a critical skill for telecommuters. They must recognize the need for, feel comfortable with, and be committed to communicating regularly with people back at the office. They must be able to do this effectively both in written form (e-mail and other written documents) and verbally (telephone, teleconference, regularly scheduled meetings).

Sample 2 — Continued

Can pace themselves to avoid both overworking and wasting time. Perhaps surprisingly, one of the common problems experienced by telecommuters is working too much. When work is always just a few steps away, it can be difficult not to succumb to the lure of doing just one more thing. Successful telecommuters are able to differentiate between work time and home time.

(Reprinted with permission from 101 Tips for Telecommuters *by Debra A. Dinnocenzo. Copyright©1999 by Debra A. Dinnocenzo.)*

SAMPLE 3
University of Michigan Telecommuting Guidelines

Employee must have a good performance record: no documented absenteeism problems and positive performance evaluations.

Employee must be able to provide an appropriate telecommuting work environment which meets university standards.

Employee should have worked at ITD [Information Technology Division] for a minimum of one year in an on-site position. If this is not possible, the manager needs to ensure that the employee becomes familiar with ITD culture and environment.

Telecommuting is appropriate for regular full-time employees as opposed to temporary employees, unless there are extenuating circumstances.

(University of Michigan, Information Technology Division, ITD Telecommuting Task Force: <www.itd.umich.edu/telecommuting> Copyright© 2001 The Regents of The University of Michigan.)

thoroughly the employee was trained and prepared, and how exceptional the support from the workplace is. Sometimes it just doesn't work out. That's okay. In your policy or contract, recognize the possibility of failure and clearly indicate what happens when the situation does not prove to be successful. Address such issues as—

- How long will the trial period be?
- What criteria will be used to determine the success of the arrangement?
- Will the telecommuter be able to terminate the arrangement? Under what circumstances?

- Will the telecommuter's manager be able to terminate the arrangement? Under what circumstances?
- Will the telecommuter be able to return to his or her traditional position? In what instances might this not be possible?

Both manager and telecommuter should thoroughly review the potential for the arrangement to prove unacceptable before the employee begins telecommuting.

At CIGNA, Susan Thomas says, each telecommuter has an agreement that lists provisions for an unsuccessful telecommuting situation. "We reserve the right to amend, modify, or terminate the arrangement at any time," she says. "People know what they're getting into."

5.2 It's not fair!

The ability to work from home is frequently viewed as a benefit by employees — particularly by those who do not have this option. This is a very real issue and one that should be considered and addressed.

Having clearly established criteria and a well-defined process for the selection of telecommuters can help prevent problems related to perceived inequities or favoritism. At Sprint, the employee's manager makes the decision of whether or not an employee is able to telecommute. "It's made very clear that this is not a right," Alan Coleman says, "it's a management alternative."

Susan Thomas agrees that these issues can be successfully addressed through clearly defined selection criteria and a well-communicated process. "It's like any other decision," she points out. "An analogy might be if you have three people in a department who apply for a specific job — one gets it and the other two don't. As long as you have a concrete reason why, there shouldn't be a problem. The employees may be disappointed, but at least they'll understand."

5.3 My manager won't let me!

Managers need to be receptive to the concept of telecommuting. Problems can develop if one manager allows his or her employees to telecommute and a manager with similar types of employees doesn't.

Alan Coleman admits that this can be a problem, even for a company like Sprint, which has embraced the concept of telecommuting

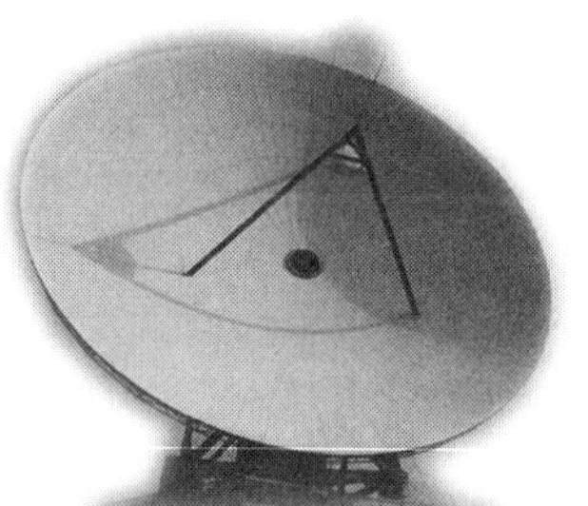

Nancy Cornelison says of her telecommuting position: "At home, I have found that I am much more creative, time-efficient, and productive than I ever was in the office."

and has been practicing telecommuting for quite some time. "One of the biggest challenges companies face is that the corporate mindset today still has visual supervision built in — getting over that is difficult. As people become more reliant on technology, that will fade, but right now, it's still prevailing."

What does he do to address this issue? Nobody at Sprint is forced to participate in telecommuting, but the development of extensive guides and assessments is encouraging. The other key, he says, is that "it absolutely requires top, executive-level support for the culture to shift. It has to be communicated through the entire organization."

6. Case Study

Nancy Cornelison is director of marketing for the Central Credit Union of Illinois. She started working for Central in March 1996. In March 1997, her husband accepted a medical residency in northern Virginia, and Cornelison told her CEO that she would be leaving. Her CEO, hesitant to lose her, made a counter proposal: How about telecommuting? Cornelison could work from her home in Virginia and travel to Chicago as needed once or twice a month. She was, she says, initially hesitant. "Because I enjoy being around people, I wasn't sure that I would find working from a home office to be rewarding." She was wrong.

Two and a half years after moving to Virginia, she says, "my responsibilities are no different than they were when I lived locally to the credit union and went to the office each day." Cornelison manages all of the credit union's marketing functions from her home office and travels to the Chicago area at least monthly to attend meetings, interact with staff, and perform various functions. She communicates regularly with the office and Chicago-based vendors by phone, fax, and e-mail. What is, perhaps, most impressive about Cornelison's telecommuting arrangement is that she is, herself, a manager. Her department consists of an assistant and a business development manager, who both work at the head office.

From a personal standpoint, she says, one of the greatest benefits has been the opportunity to continue working in a position that she finds personally and professionally rewarding. But the benefits don't end there: "I feel the credit union has benefited significantly from this arrangement," says Cornelison. "It is amazing how distracting an office environment can be when you're trying to accomplish certain tasks. At home, I have found that I am much more creative, time-efficient, and productive than I ever was in the office."

She admits, though, that telecommuting isn't for everyone. "A lot of people ask me how I motivate myself to work when I'm at home. It takes a lot of personal discipline to work out of your home which, like an office, can have a lot of distractions. Fortunately, I am motivated to perform by the goals that I have set for myself." And, she adds, "for people like me, one of the most difficult challenges of telecommuting isn't working in your home office — it's leaving it at the end of the day!"

Chapter 5
RECRUITING TELECOMMUTERS

"We're at a point in time where we're seeing a fundamental change in the way that work gets done in the world."

— Rick Davis
CEO of online job marketplace Ants.com

Executive Summary

Do telecommuters always come from existing staff?

Not always. While the majority of companies that offer telecommuting as an option to employees do hire from within, there are a growing number of examples of companies that are actually recruiting individuals to serve as telecommuters. One of the key benefits of recruiting individuals to work in telecommuting arrangements is that they can literally be located anywhere. This enlarges the labor pool for employers who are, increasingly, operating in a tight labor market.

How can I effectively recruit employees from diverse geographic locations?

The Internet has opened up a wealth of opportunities for employers when recruiting staff of almost any kind. There are a number of recruitment sites online that offer employers, at minimal or no cost, the opportunity to promote open positions and/or to review résumés that have been posted by job seekers. Your own Web site can also be a good way to promote open positions.

Isn't it risky to hire people sight unseen?

Not necessarily. Consider that some professions have been doing this for decades; freelance writers, for instance, are frequently hired to write for publications, and may never actually meet the editors with whom they are working. The key is to focus on the requirements of the position and to look for evidence that the candidate can meet those requirements (just as when hiring for any traditional position). Also, just because you are hiring for a telecommuting position doesn't mean that you shouldn't ask the candidates to come to your office for in-person interviews.

What if I make the wrong choice?

What if you make the wrong choice in any hiring situation? Not every candidate will work out and, when this happens, you would follow the steps you would normally follow in terminating any employee.

Is it more important to check the references of candidates for telecommuting positions?

No, but it is equally important. Reference checking is a critical step in any recruitment process. Make sure that you take the time to thoroughly review any applicant's background by contacting past employers and, where possible, speaking with others who may have experience and insights related to the applicant's ability to perform the job.

RECRUITING TELECOMMUTERS

Most organizations that use telecommuters select them from their existing workforce. Face it: That's the least risky thing to do. You are familiar with these people. They've proven their worth, their commitment, and their efficiency. But what if you really don't have anybody on staff that you feel would be suitable for the position? Worse, what if you're looking for certain skills or experience that just don't seem to exist in your geographic area? Or, as seems to be the case more often these days, what if your organization isn't a brick-and-mortar facility and you don't really care where your employees live, just as long as they can do the job?

Gil Gordon, a widely recognized expert on telecommuting, says that while the "reality today is that the majority of companies select telecommuters from their current workforce, I think that's beginning to change slowly. The nature of the employment relationship is changing overall, with a shift to more use of contractors and consultants and the advent of the so-called virtual organization. It's no longer assumed that the worker needs to be on-site full-time."

One of the real benefits of hiring individuals as telecommuters is that they don't have to live anywhere near your business. Your hiring pool is infinitely large. But the sheer size of this pool can also present a disadvantage when it comes to recruiting. Where do you begin?

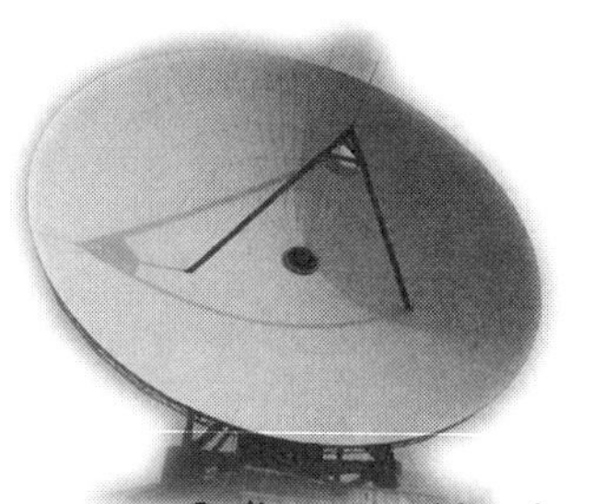

Online recruiting is growing exponentially. Finding employees online allows an employer to reach a much broader audience.

The traditional recruitment option — placing a classified ad in your local newspaper — may limit your search unnecessarily. Networking may be equally limited, depending on the geographic scope and background of the people you know. Job fairs may or may not work. In short, the traditional means that have worked for other positions may not work as well when you're recruiting individuals for telecommuting positions.

Fortunately, there are numerous online recruitment sites available. Some of the more popular sites include Monster Board (www.monster.com), Nation Job (www.nationjob.com), and Career Mosaic (www.careermosaic.com). There are hundreds of others.

In fact, online recruiting is growing exponentially. A 1998 American Management Association survey of HR professionals showed growth of 353 percent in online recruiting from 1997, with 59 percent of the respondents indicating that they use online recruiting and another 13 percent indicating that they plan to implement it soon. Seventy percent of the HR personnel surveyed indicated that they use the Internet for job postings — that compares to only 21 percent in 1996.

Rick Davis, CEO of an online job marketplace called Ants.com, says, "We're at a point in time where we're seeing a fundamental change in the way that work gets done in the world." He points to three trends: the movement of companies from "insourcing to outsourcing," the growing number of people whose incomes are shifting from "W2 permanent jobs to 1099 work," and the "huge trend from local employment to global employment." The Internet, he says, "has come along at a point in time where it's the perfect medium for finding people who can do the kind of work that you need to get done as quickly as you need to get it done."

1. The Internet As a Recruiting Tool

While the large job boards like Monster Board appeal to the masses, there are a number of industry-specific sites that can help you narrow your search. Sites such as <www.showbizjobs.com>, <www.salesengineer.com>, and <www.healthopps.com> provide both employers and job seekers with the ability to narrowly target their searches.

Obviously, not all of the online job seekers are looking for telecommuting opportunities. Still, the Internet has been a definite boost both for telecommuters looking for work and for the employers who are looking for them.

The best way to become familiar with the recruiting resources available on the Internet is to review the various services yourself, keeping in mind that you want to find one that is most advantageous for you. Smaller, more specialized services may be more appropriate for your needs, depending on the type of position you are attempting to fill. Just as when you are recruiting through more traditional means, using a combination of resources can be the best way to promote your telecommuting job openings.

Before posting an online ad, research the site to make sure it matches the position you're advertising. For example, don't try to find a computer programmer on a job site devoted to telemarketers.

1.1 Online recruiting sites

There are countless online recruiting sites — with more being developed on a virtually daily basis! Some are devoted specifically to job searches. A quick and easy way to find out information about the latest online job sites is to conduct a search using one of the many online search engines. The following is a list of some of the more popular sites, and those most directly suited to employers seeking telecommuters. This list is not meant to be exhaustive, and given the rapidly changing nature of the Internet, some sites may have been discontinued or renamed by the time this is published.

Ants.com (www.ants.com)

At Ants.com, companies can outsource jobs and request competitive bids from what is being billed as "the largest online community of qualified independent contractors and freelance workers in the world." Ants.com boasts 16,000 members and more than 30 categories of job descriptions. "Regardless of location, Ants.com will bring people together to get the work done," says president and CEO Rick Davis.

Ants.com works on a "reverse auction" model, says Davis. A company that needs help will answer a few questions, then the people looking for work will seek them out. Based on the criteria the prospective employer lists, Ants.com will send an e-mail to those job seekers who have indicated that they are appropriate for and/or interested in the type of work being offered.

CareerPath.com (www.careerpath.com)

CareerPath.com is an online job site that draws from the classified print advertisements of newspapers throughout the United States. For an additional charge from the newspaper, the classified ad is automatically posted on CareerPath, where, according to its promotional materials, such ads are searched nearly 3.5 million times each month. CareerPath.com's research indicates that the vast majority of searches (40.1 percent) are conducted for technical jobs (computer, engineering, and telecommunications).

Guru.com (www.guru.com)

Guru.com's tagline is "Power for the independent professional." Employers have the option of searching posted résumés, many including salary requirements, or posting job openings of their own. Posting an open position on this site is a simple, five-step process. An added feature here is an interface that allows employers to keep track of multiple postings and lists of top leads for each job posted. In addition to job postings, the Guru.com site offers online articles, information Q&As, and discussion forums.

The site is relatively new (launched in January 2000), and at the time of writing there was no charge for using its services. However, the user agreement states, "At this time Accounts are provided to Hirers for free. You agree that we may charge for the use of certain features of your Account (such as posting gigs) and/or additional premium services offered in the future and that you will be responsible for all charges (including tax) for using such additional services if you choose to continue use. You will be notified of any changes and given an option to continue use or to terminate your Account."

The Independent Homeworkers Alliance (www.homeworkers.org)

The Independent Homeworkers Alliance (IHA) is a site devoted specifically to telecommuting and freelance jobs. The site combines a jobs database (with more than 55,000 jobs) and automated résumé submission service with access to information and training materials.

The following notice for a virtual recruiter appeared at the IHA site in early 2000:

> **Virtual Recruiter — US**
>
> **Location: US — Nationwide**
>
> Fast growing technical recruiting agency based in New York City is looking for "virtual recruiters" who want to work from home (or anywhere, for that matter). Scour the Internet, search job boards, screen applicants, generate sales leads. Any knowledge of technical lingo is a plus. This is a commission-paid position only. Must be Internet savvy. Can be extremely profitable for the right candidate. Recruiting experience is a plus.

Applicants using the IHA site, unlike those using services like Monster Board (below), must pay a monthly fee to respond to job postings ($24.96 in January 2000).

Monster Board (www.monster.com)

Monster.com memberships allow employers to post jobs in real time, and to access more than one million résumés that are stored in the Monster database (and that are searchable by various criteria). Starter memberships contain 15 – 60 jobs and are designed for smaller companies that only require résumé database access for up to five users. Full memberships contain 60 – 1000 jobs and are designed for medium-sized, large, or fast-growing companies that require an enterprise-wide solution for 10 – 50 résumé database users or more. Pricing varies, but to give a general idea of the cost, a single 60-day US job posting cost $275 in early 2000. Employers may use Monster.com to post openings as well as complete company profiles. The site also offers a résumé screening service as well as routing and searching. An online template makes it easy to develop an online listing.

Ironically, the inherent downfall may be the sheer size of Monster.com and the associated potential for your listings to be lost in the clutter.

Workaholics 4 Hire (www.workaholics4hire.com)

The Workaholics4hire.com site offers a database of telecommuting and work-at-home jobs that is accessible at no up-front charges. However, if job seekers are successful, they pay a commission to the site based on 10 percent of their net salary for six months — or, for the duration of any arrangement that is shorter than six months.

An online template is provided to make it easy for job posters to submit applicable information, including sections intended to detail their home-office equipment and software: "Enter a detailed list of the software you have on your computer. Make sure you enter all software, including those freeware programs. Don't just say Microsoft Office, list all components separately. This an essential piece of information for your telecommuting résumé."

As an employer, simply enter some keywords to pull up summaries of various online applicants. Click to see complete résumés. Then e-mail the job candidate (through workaholics4hire.com) to indicate your interest.

1.2 Effective online recruiting

If you're recruiting online, you need to have the same familiarity with these services as you would with any technical or professional journal in which you were advertising. Who are the users of the site? What are their characteristics? How frequently is the site accessed? How widely do they advertise? Is the profession for which you are recruiting well represented?

The use of key words — the search words that online job seekers will enter to pull up your listing — is a critical and often overlooked skill. You need to tie the appropriate key words to your ads. And you need to probe to make sure that your ads are being properly coded. If you have posted ads and wonder why you are not receiving any inquiries, the coding process may be the culprit. Each search engine is different, and you need to take the time to learn how each one functions and what sort of patterns there are in putting the key words together. You don't want to code too restrictively or too broadly. Knowledge of how terminology is used in the field from which you're recruiting is a must.

A good way to become familiar with the technology is to practice with your own résumé or advertisement. This will give you insight into how easy or difficult it is to access the online résumés of qualified candidates — or how easy it is for candidates to find your ad. If you post your résumé or ad to a service and it is not pulled up when you enter the key words that you feel are most relevant, something is wrong.

The following sample ad provides an extensive amount of useful detail about the position it describes:

Being very specific in your online job posting will help you to eliminate as many undesirable applicants as possible before moving on to the interviewing process.

> **Telecommuting Project Manager**
>
> **(WASH. DC AREA ONLY!)**
>
> You know you want to telecommute. You've been reading *Dilbert* for years, you have no patience with the corporate world, and what you really want is to manage projects, write documents, and make the world a better place, from your home, in your bathrobe. Or you have kids — little ones — and you want to spend time with them. Or you're retired but are bored out of your skull, and you were a crack C programmer in your day.
>
> Turner Consulting Group is seeking a full-time project manager to work with clients and TCG staff to lead the creation of additional award-winning Web applications. This is a W-2/W-4 position, not a 1099 or contract position.
>
> A TCG project manager is the liaison between TCG and the client, managing the relationship on a day-to-day basis and keeping both sides informed about changes in desires, wishes, and possibilities. It is the project manager's job to understand what the client wants (even when the client is unsure) and to convey that to the programmers, interfacers, documenters, and quality-assurance staff at TCG — and to make sure that the client's needs are met by the TCG product. The job involves face to face communication, a great deal of written communication, and all electronic forms of communication, so the Project Manager needs to be facile with all of them. The project manager is ultimately accountable for the success of the project, and is given the responsibility needed to succeed. Because TCG is not a top-down organization, negotiation skills are often needed in project development. As most TCG clients are in the Washington, DC, area, Project Managers should also be in the Washington, DC, area to be

available to meet with them a few times a week. However, Project Managers — like all TCG employees — work from home, so when you are not meeting with clients you control where you work and what you do. (TCG employees are hourly, and are limited to working a maximum of 40 hours a week.)

TCG project managers are expected to have many of the following skills and experience (* indicates a requirement; others are optional):

- * good communication skills
- * a clue about Web site development
- ability to write successful proposals
- a track record in establishing priorities, meeting deadlines, and managing a team in a complicated task
- experience in resource planning and keeping a project on budget
- understanding of risk management, problem solving, change requests, and project scope
- experience writing technical specifications, including database schematics and script specifications
- experience with large projects as a developer, architect, or project leader
- knowledge of psychology
- knowledge of usability testing
- experience in testing and quality-assurance
- knowledge of HTML or programming (particularly C, Perl, and SQL)
- knowledge of servers, software, and security on the Web
- understanding of design, coding, testing, integration, and implementation of Web applications
- a degree in engineering, computer science, information systems, or telecommunications

- a graduate degree in any of the above, or an MBA
- knowledge of Windows, MacOS, NT, MSProject, Excel, or UNIX
- * facility with picking up buzzwords like "solutions," "tasking," and "OOP" and the ability to explain a project without using any of them
- * ability to read fine print, read from a computer monitor, review documents, use a keyboard, dial a telephone, and sit for extended periods in meetings and at the computer.
- * ability to communicate effectively and prudently by e-mail

It is also important to be able to laugh at yourself.

We pay competitive wages and we offer much better benefits than you'll get as a contract employee. We have a 401k and a health plan, including dental and vision benefits.

Please contact pmjobs@TCG-inc.com with a resume in MS Word, Postscript, HTML, or ASCII text. If you are unable to communicate via e-mail, we are not interested in you. Naturally, Turner Consulting Group does not discriminate on the basis of race, sex, color, religion, national origin, age, disability, veteran status, or anything else that makes you part of any group. We discriminate on the basis of talent, ability, and experience. Try us...we'll make you happy.

(Copyright© 1999 by Turner Consulting Group, <http://www.TCG-inc.com/>)

This may seem like a lot of information, but that level of detail and specificity is critical whenever recruiting — and particularly when recruiting online. There are literally thousands of individuals searching online job sites for positions. While a very general posting may provide you with countless leads, the more specific you can be, the more clearly you can narrow the market to only those candidates who are uniquely qualified to fill the positions you have available.

"The goal," says Rick Davis of Ants.com, is for "companies to reduce the transaction cost and get the best people, no matter where they are. The well is infinitely deep for people who want to post projects;

the community is so big that, invariably, somebody will have the skills that will meet your needs."

1.3 Using your own Web site

Another rich source of applicants for many organizations is their own Web sites. In fact, according to Katie Atkinson, President of Results Direct Internet Marketing, "In general, job listings are consistently the most popular by virtue of the subject matter, if you will — that's going to draw people."

If you have a Web site already, consider adding a section detailing your vacant positions. Make your Web site user friendly by offering job seekers the ability to search by key words, location, job title, or pay. Include the option to apply for positions or submit résumés online. Again, being specific and detailed is important. Consider these listings your one opportunity to attract the attention of interested applicants.

Of course, simply including job listings on your site isn't enough to generate response. You need to make sure that potential job seekers know that this information is available. That means promoting your site. Atkinson recommends to clients that they use Rolodex cards or post-it notes with their Web address and take advantage of other traditional print media (i.e., direct mail, notices on statements, etc.). Include your Web address in all your traditional employment advertisements. "It's really a matter of being consistent about your marketing and using a number of different vehicles to market," Atkinson says.

Most important, make sure that your listings are up to date, and that you're responsive to the inquiries that you do receive.

2. Other Sources of Applicants

New media aren't the only source of job applicants when searching for telecommuters. The traditional media may work well, depending on your specific needs. Placing classified ads in local newspapers or running ads in related trade journals can be effective ways of reaching potential telecommuting candidates. In fact, Tom Joseph, president and CEO of Bookminders, a company that provides bookkeeping services with a staff made up exclusively of home-based workers, uses classified ads in the local paper to attract candidates. He's been so successful using this traditional recruiting source that he's reached the point where he actually has an overabundance of applicants. In an era in which unemployment rates are at all-time lows, his success in attracting candidates speaks well for the growing interest in flexible work options. "We're attracting people who want to work out of their homes, which is a lot of people," Joseph says. "We've come to see our recruiting as a sort of filtering process."

Although using the Internet can certainly help you to reach a broad pool of talent, don't abandon traditional methods such as newspaper classified ads, job fairs, and employee referrals.

Other sources of applicants include:

- *Job fairs.* Job fairs are becoming an increasingly popular source of job candidates. Generally organized by industry, job fairs are like trade shows that provide employers with the opportunity to meet interested job seekers in a particular field. For instance, a community might sponsor a small-manufacturing job fair at which area manufacturers would be present to provide information on their companies and their personnel needs.
- *Recruitment open houses.* This is an approach that Joseph also uses, and it has been extremely successful for him. "We bring in 20–30 people a month to screen," he says. Holding an open house for your own company provides you with the opportunity to present your job openings exclusively to a group of interested job candidates.
- *Recommendations and referrals.* Referrals from your existing employees can be a great source of potential telecommuting candidates. These referrals can generally be trusted — after all, the employee has a vested interest in seeing the referral work out.

Rather than relying on any one source for applicants, use a combination of means to generate interest. Whatever means you use, be sure to clearly outline your needs and expectations. The recruitment stage is the critical first step toward ensuring that your telecommuters will be capable and productive.

3. Steps in the Hiring Process

Whether advertising in the local paper or running an ad on Monster.com, the hiring process you use for telecommuters will be much the same as for any employee.

Carol Stein of the Internet research company HR Library says, "I've hired everybody off the 'net." She posts job descriptions in "librarian-type mailing lists." Every aspect of the interaction between the applicant and Stein is used as part of the selection process. Part of that process, Stein says, is watching how the applicant follows directions. For example, Stein's ads say that the résumé should be included in the body of the e-mail. Applicants who send résumés as attachments are immediately disqualified. For the type of job she's filling, Stein says, attention to detail and the ability to use the Internet and technology effectively — and precisely — are very important.

For those who submit their résumés according to Stein's instructions, the next step is a sample research project. If they pass that hurdle, applicants are flown to Tampa to meet Stein in person. "It's just like hiring anybody else," she stresses. "You just have to look at what your criteria are — but the hiring practice isn't any different."

3.1 Position requirements

As with any position, your first step in hiring a telecommuter will be determining the requirements of the position. This will not only help you make an informed decision, but will also help narrow your choices in terms of recruitment vehicles. The Internet Business Network, a research firm based in Mill Valley, California, estimates that the Web has more than 100,000 job-related sites — and 2.5 million résumés — online. Before you begin your search, you should consider the following:

- *Education.* What level of education is necessary to perform effectively in the position? High school? College? Special training? Will job performance require any type of special certificate or license?
- *Experience.* How much previous, related experience should a new employee have? Will training be offered on the job? Experience and education requirements are often tied together; for example, "Bachelor's degree plus a minimum of three years' experience in the field."
- *Personality requirements.* As discussed in chapter 4, there are specific personality traits that differentiate those who will perform effectively as telecommuters from those who will not be successful in this role.

As you put together your list of requirements, make sure that each is specifically job related to avoid claims or charges of discrimination. Don't make these job determinations in a vacuum. Ask other members of the organization for their perspectives.

Outlining your expectations before hiring an individual will allow you to evaluate his or her performance fairly.

Be specific. Communication is a critical element in any telecommuting relationship, and it starts during recruitment. You should have a very clear understanding of what the job will entail and the specific requirements of the position. Job descriptions and job specifications are two tools that can greatly help you in this process.

The job description provides a written record of the qualifications required for the position and outlines how the job relates to others in the company. It should include—

- position title,
- salary or pay grade,
- department,
- to whom the position is accountable,
- hours required,
- job summary,
- major responsibilities or tasks,
- qualifications, and
- relation of the position to others in the company.

The job description should be organized in such a way that it indicates not only the responsibilities involved, but also the relative importance of these responsibilities. The telecommuting job description should also indicate how the telecommuter will interact with colleagues, and should discuss other issues related to the telecommuting relationship. Within the broad categories mentioned above, you will want to include such information as—

- extent of authority exercised over the position,
- level of complexity of the duties performed,
- amount of internal and external contact (including any requirements for on-site meetings),

- amount of access to confidential information,
- amount of independent judgment required,
- amount of pressure involved in the job,
- type of equipment used (and how that equipment will be purchased and maintained),
- working conditions (including expectations for the home office environment), and
- terms of employment.

Job specifications are another useful tool in the recruitment process. Job specifications describe the personal qualifications that are required for a job and include any special conditions of employment. In the case of telecommuting, this may include such things as required hours of availability and responsibility for maintaining equipment.

Some key questions to ask yourself as you are preparing a position description are the following:

- What is the purpose of the job?
- What day-to-day duties are performed?
- How is the position supervised?
- What other positions receive supervision from this position?
- How much, or how little, control is exercised over this position?
- What machines or equipment must be operated?
- What types of records need to be kept by this position?
- To what extent is this position involved in analysis and planning?
- What internal and external contacts are required of this position?
- What verbal, numerical, or mechanical aptitudes are required?

3.2 Selection criteria

On what evidence will you base your hiring decision? There are three commonly used selection measures for evaluating job applicants, including self-report, direct observation, and work samples. You may decide to use one or a combination of all three.

Self-report is the most commonly used measure. You ask the applicant about their accomplishments and experience, and they provide you with information — information that is, by its very nature, subject to bias.

Direct observation, although often not possible, allows you to actually observe the candidate doing the work you will require. To approximate this measure, you might —

- use one of many tests that have been developed to measure various skills and abilities,
- role-play certain tasks (i.e., sales calls, telemarketing scripts, etc.), or
- use hypothetical questions or situations to approximate real-life situations.

Work samples are appropriate for a number of positions that might lend themselves to telecommuting (i.e., computer programmers, Website developers, writers, graphic designers).

The job specifications that you used to begin your job search will play a major role in helping you make a final decision. Applicants should be evaluated both in terms of how well they meet the job specifications and how they compare to other applicants. For this reason, it is important to reserve a final decision until all interviews have been completed. Don't make a decision after each interview. It is best to wait until all interviews are completed and then rate interviewees on the basis of the criteria you have determined are the best predictors of job performance.

The selection process is subjective, leaving many areas open to bias and error. If you are aware of the possibility for error, you have taken one of the first steps to becoming a fair evaluator of job applicants. The following points can help make this demanding task a little less intimidating:

- Be prepared
- Identify desired behaviors in observable rather than subjective terms
- Be aware of your own personal biases and work to overcome them
- Try using more than one interviewer and comparing results to determine possible bias
- Don't assume that excellence in one area implies excellence in all areas
- Base judgments on demonstrated performance, not anticipated performance

3.3 Interviewing telecommuting candidates

Interviewing candidates for telecommuting can be done far more conveniently and creatively than one might imagine. For example, your first interview might actually take place online, via e-mail. After all, if this is the means by which you will most frequently communicate with your telecommuting employee, doesn't it make sense to get a good idea of their skills in this medium up front? From there, you may want to go on to a telephone interview. Eventually, but not always, you may want to bring the candidate into your office.

The interview process will be much the same as the process for hiring any employee. Focus on the criteria you've established for the position and develop questions designed to determine if the candidates have the experience, background, and personal traits and characteristics that will enable them to be successful telecommuters.

Your goal is to identify behaviors that will lead to successful job performance and to devise questions that let you determine if applicants will be a good fit. "Project yourself into the future," Rick Davis of Ants.com suggests. "Look back and describe the ideal outcome. This gives you a sense of what a good person to hire 'looks like.' "

When you ask questions of your telecommuting candidates, you want to gather as much information as possible and probe for meaningful responses. Your interviewing skills will determine whether or not you gather all the pertinent information.

While there are never any guarantees that the person you hire will work out, a well-conducted interview will improve your chances of making an informed decision.

Since about one third of all job applicants alter their résumés or misrepresent their qualifications, it is vital that you take the time to check references.

3.4 References

About a third of all job candidates alter their résumés or misrepresent their qualifications when applying for a job.

Ninety percent of all hiring mistakes can be prevented through proper reference-checking procedures. Unfortunately, countless employers neglect this important step in the hiring process. They rely instead on their own impressions of the candidate based on the résumé, application, and interview. This is a major mistake and it can be a costly one. Checking the references of your telecommuting applicants is absolutely essential to obtain accurate information about their qualifications and experience.

Many employers call references after interviews have been conducted. Making these calls beforehand can help you filter out undesirable candidates earlier, saving time that you would have spent in an interview. Checking references before the interview can also provide you with additional areas to explore during the interview, and can help you formulate pertinent questions in advance.

Before checking references, prepare questions and have a clear idea of the information you hope to obtain. You will want to ask questions related to the applicant's ability to work independently, to be productive, and to achieve results. Keep in mind that some organizations have policies against giving a great deal of information about former or current employees and will provide little detail beyond length of service and rate of pay. Still, it pays to be persistent and to ask for additional sources of information along the way. Try asking, "Is there anyone else I should speak with?"

Try these questions when checking references:

- What was the quality of the applicant's work?

- How much direction did the applicant need?
- Did the applicant consistently meet deadlines?
- How were the applicant's problem-solving skills?
- Tell me about the applicant's communication skills.
- In your opinion, is this a person who can work well in a telecommuting position with minimal supervision?

4. Perils and Pitfalls

Any hiring decision is important, but when hiring telecommuters, you must be particularly vigilant. Because you will be relying upon them to be self-sufficient and reliable, you need to make sure that you take the time to clearly identify the type of candidate you need, to interview carefully, to check references, and to make hiring decisions based on objective criteria. There are a number of potential perils and pitfalls that you should be aware of as you go through this process:

- *Not adapting your processes and procedures to the online environment.* The world is changing, technology is changing, and your hiring practices need to change too. Many of the steps you have taken in the past will not convert readily — or efficiently — to online venues. Be flexible and willing to adapt whenever necessary.
- *Limiting yourself to one or two sources of applicants.* Don't give up on traditional sources of recruiting, such as newspapers or trade journals. Take advantage of the plethora of recruitment sites, and keep up with the new additions. Be adventurous and be constantly alert to new online opportunities.
- *Overlooking local or regional sites.* Local communities frequently have job-site listings at chamber of commerce or local newspaper sites. If you're located in Minnesota, but want to tap into the technological expertise you believe exists in San Francisco, check out some of the local San Francisco sites in addition to the major national sites.

- *Not using the sites yourself.* The best way to learn about recruitment over the Internet is to actively visit and use the various sites. As a user you can test the search capabilities, posting opportunities, content, and general usability of these sites.
- *Comparing apples to oranges.* One of the benefits — and downfalls — of the Internet is that even the least experienced and least reputable organizations can develop sites that present a "Wow!" image. Don't be too easily taken in by the glamorous front. Carefully consider the types of postings the site offers, the number of postings, and the charges (direct and hidden) before making any decision to pay for services.

5. Case Study

Bookminders, Inc. was founded in 1991 to provide outsourced bookkeeping services to 150 companies and nonprofits, and has drawn much attention as a model for telecommuting success. Bookminders is unique, in a sense, because it was conceived with the intention that "home-based workers would drive" the business.

Bookminders targets small- to medium-sized businesses that require at least part-time bookkeeping support. The company offers all the benefits of an in-house computer bookkeeping department without the support burden or cost overhead, and serves more than 150 different businesses, including contractors, consultants, restaurants, retailers, manufacturers, medical professionals, lawyers, nonprofits, and property managers.

All 40 of Bookminders' employees work from home and telecommute via fax and e-mail. Most are women with young children who work between 20 and 40 hours a week. The home of each employee is equipped with hardware, software, and telecommunications equipment that links the workforce with the corporate office. Tom Joseph, founder and CEO of Bookminders, doesn't call what his employees do telecommuting, but the concepts are similar.

Joseph says that through trial and error, he believes he has found a process that works for finding employees. The extensive amount of training and orientation involved for Bookminders staff means that the investment of time in any one employee can be substantial. Joseph can't afford to have high turnover. Consequently, he must make sure that his hiring practices are sound.

Because Tom Joseph, CEO of Bookminders, receives an overabundance of résumés, he has developed an extensive recruitment process designed to ensure that only the best-suited applicants are hired.

It all starts with an ad in the local newspaper. Ads are run each month and generally elicit 20 to 30 applicants. Applicants are invited to an open house — a structured event — where, Joseph says, "we basically try to talk them out of working for us." The reasons are simple. According to Joseph, unlike many businesses, he does not suffer from a lack of job applicants. On the contrary, he receives an overabundance of résumés. He has found that to reduce the applicants to a chosen few, it is important to first of all be very specific in the recruitment ads; second, to clearly outline to prospective employees what the requirements of the job will be; and third, to implement a process of testing designed to weed through the remaining applicants. In fact, Joseph says, anywhere from one-third to one-half of his applicants are not able to pass the tests he gives — and those applicants are accounting professionals with college degrees and three to five years of experience.

Joseph wants only the best candidates, so the application process must be rigorous. "If our recruiting process isn't working, it's expensive," he says. "That's why we put a ton of time into this process."

Chapter 6
TRAINING TELECOMMUTERS AND THEIR MANAGERS

"[Training] improve[s] the quality of the telecommuting program by taking the guesswork out of remote work."

— Gil Gordon
Founder of consulting firm Gil Gordon Associates

Executive Summary

Is training really necessary?

Training is critical! Don't stop with just training telecommuters. Training should also be offered for managers — and even for non-telecommuting employees who will be required to interact with telecommuting staff.

How much training should I offer?

Enough to cover the key points — to provide the telecommuter and other trainees with the information they need to be successful. Training times vary from 1- to 2-hour sessions to 1- to 3-day sessions. It all depends on your particular situation. The key is not to skimp on training.

Do managers need training?

Yes. In fact, in addition to individual sessions, it's a good idea to offer an opportunity for managers and employees to have the opportunity to spend time with each other to discuss the details of the arrangement.

Can managers really be trained to supervise telecommuters?

Yes. While the skills required to manage telecommuters are very similar to those required to manage any employee, there are specific techniques and interactions that are unique to this relationship. Chief among these is the ability to manage based on outcomes rather than on process. Managers need to become comfortable with the concept of managing employees who are not physically present. The establishment of clear expectations and frequent communication become a critical part of this relationship. These are issues that can be successfully dealt with through training and education.

Is an initial training session sufficient?

It's a good start. Refresher sessions can be helpful, particularly as technology changes. Other issues (work schedules, goals, etc.) should be covered regularly as part of your normal evaluation and review process.

Can training be done online?

Yes. Opinions vary on whether this is optimum, but it is certainly possible. You may also wish to consider putting useful reference materials online for quick and easy access by remote workers.

TRAINING TELECOMMUTERS AND THEIR MANAGERS

A 1998 survey by Kensington Technology Group, a leader in the design and sales of computer accessories, indicated that 63 percent of employers do not provide formal training or manuals on how to telecommute productively. In a survey conducted by the American Management Association (AMA) in 1999, only 7 percent of the telecommuters at US-based corporations had been formally trained to work outside their normal office environment, based on responses from the 1,265 executives surveyed.

"While companies and workers are readily embracing telecommuting, many employers are not taking on the responsibility of properly equipping, training, or providing protections for their telecommuters," says Dr. Charlie Grantham of the Institute for the Study of Distributed Work, which offers consulting services for Fortune 500 companies entering the alternative work world.

"This is really a leadership opportunity for employers," Grantham says. "As the workplace becomes more mobile, employers need to think about extending support to telecommuters — not just from a productivity standpoint, but also to address liability questions and to stay ahead of guidelines that may be otherwise legislated."

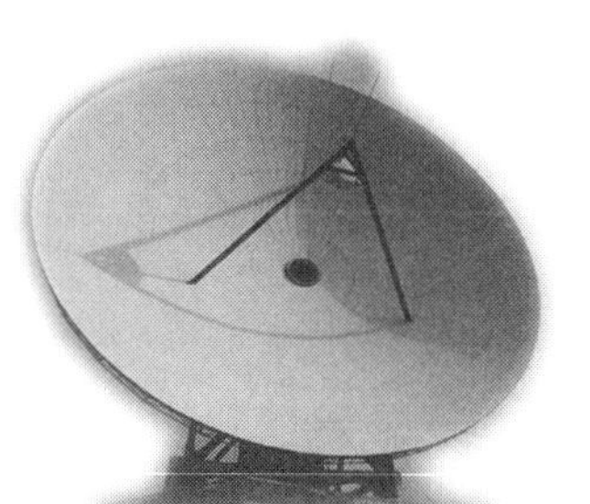
To make a telecommuting program successful, a training program should be developed as soon as possible.

To be most effective, training should be part of the telecommuting program's development from the conceptual stage. This means that you are already well on your way to having a solid training program. George Piskurich, author of *An Organizational Guide to Telecommuting* (ASTD, 1998), says that in the act of conceptualizing a telecommuting program and defining policies and procedures to institute in your company, you have already taken a major step in creating a solid training program. He maintains that "those policies and procedures — what they are, what they mean, and how to work within them — are 50 percent to 60 percent of the training."

Successful telecommuting programs require successful training. At Merrill Lynch, as at most companies with effective telecommuting programs, this means formalized training. In many of these companies, training is broken down into three parts: telecommuter training, supervisor/manager training, and "team training" — an opportunity for the telecommuter and his or her manager to come together and discuss the issues that impact the relationship. This three-tiered training structure is an essential tool for implementing and maintaining a telecommuting program that works. Let's have a closer look at how these three facets of training operate.

1. Telecommuter Training

Telecommuting doesn't just happen because an employee who used to work in the office now works from home. It's not quite that simple. There are certain differences between working at the head office and working at home. Those differences need to be covered through training and orientation to ensure that the telecommuter knows what to expect and is capable of making the transition.

1.1 Characteristics of telecommuter training programs

Telecommuting training programs generally have the following characteristics:

- Individual sessions are conducted for telecommuters and their managers; both groups are brought together at some point to participate in planning and general discussion.

- Technology is an element of training, but it takes a back seat to more critical issues such as a heavy emphasis on communication skills, establishment of measurable goals, and discussion of how to measure progress.
- A focus on some of the "softer" issues such as how to deal with interruptions at home and how to handle isolation, and a sharing of experiences are important parts of the training process.

Steve Schilling emphasizes that training needs to go beyond technology training to address the human issues of telecommuting.

Dr. Richard A. Skinner, president of Clayton College & State University and the Metropolitan Atlanta Telecommuting Advisory Council, says, "We've found that the training begins with the workers and managers together initially so they all hear the same thing. We've found that small groups work best — about 20 people. And we've found that what we call the sharing opportunity — people talking through their experiences — is important. I call this testimonial time. You can have all of the slick films and presentation you want, but what people want to hear are authentic voices."

Steve Schilling of TeleCommute Solutions says that a mistake that many companies make when it comes to telecommuting training is that they "train on technology, but they don't get into the basic experience-type things or the coordination-type things. When you're implementing a telecommuting program, step one is to understand that there are a lot of issues at play beyond technology and that the cultural, managerial, and interpersonal implications of telecommuting are really much bigger than technology."

By separating technology from the core training, organizations are able to focus on more critical issues, such as communication. "Communication skills are the core," Grantham says. "When you start to substitute e-mail and voice mail for face-to-face conversations, communication gets a little bit muddier, a little bit messier."

1.2 A structure for telecommuter training

Gil Gordon has developed some training programs that are structured on some very basic principles, and have proven to be highly effective.

The training, he says, should become "institutionalized" — "as routine as any other training that you'd expect to happen normally in an organization. That means that it's offered not once, but on some regular interval." As do others, he views the role of HR as critical. "If I had my wish, the ideal training faculty would be a team: a line manager who could speak from experience, a real telecommuter, and an HR or training person. That provides the combination of real-life experience and peers talking to peers against the backdrop of a training professional."

The following is a summary of his program for telecommuters:

BRIEFING SESSION FOR PROSPECTIVE TELECOMMUTERS

PURPOSE: To help prospective telecommuters make an informed decision about whether or not they want to apply for consideration to be selected into a telecommuting pilot program. Also useful for people considering working at home in a more informal program. The objective is to make sure the people look beyond some of the obvious advantages (e.g., more flexible schedule, less formal environment, better family interaction, less commuting) and consider some of the special demands and requirements of working at home.

FORMAT: A 90-minute session that begins with a short overview about telecommuting (unless this has been provided already). Next, a short self-scoring survey to help employees identify how well they are likely to succeed as telecommuters, based on issues of suitability of the home setting, support from family members, relationship with the supervisor, and other factors.

This is followed by an interactive discussion of "Ten Key Questions" that prospective telecommuters should ask themselves about working at home, and then a candid discussion of the real and perceived career effects of working as a telecommuter. Also reviewed are the role of and content of the "telecommuter's agreement," and a series of "Next Steps" to be taken before deciding whether or not to request participation as a telecommuter.

BENEFITS TO PARTICIPANTS: This session improves the quality of the telecommuting program by:

- Helping employees who are not suited for telecommuting screen themselves out of consideration

- Helping employers keep the cost of training and equipping telecommuters down by eliminating employees who are less likely to succeed as telecommuters
- Creating enthusiasm for the telecommuting concept, while adding some much-needed reality to the myths that often exist
- The session can be run with groups of 10–30 participants; larger groups are possible but this limits the valuable discussion and interaction.

1.3 Making it real

All of the training in the world and all possible interaction with experienced telecommuters can't substitute for personal experience. The transition from office to home is a trying one for many, and companies struggle with ways to make the move less stressful and more productive.

Bernadette Fusaro is a work/life manager for Merrill Lynch, where she is responsible for the organization's alternative work programs, including telecommuting. Fusaro points to their simulation lab as a unique aspect of training that really makes a difference for employees making the transition to telecommuting. The lab is a large room that contains work stations where telecommuters work for two weeks, using the equipment that they will bring home with them. At the end of the two-week period, they're taught how to put their computers together and take them apart, then they're given the computers to take home to work. "We've found that that's been an excellent way to prepare telecommuters," Fusaro says.

Technology can definitely assist in the training process, George Piskurich says. He tells of a training program his company did with a client that involved a computer-mediated instruction process. Instead of having participants come to the classroom, they were hooked up through their company's intranet. "Trainees and instructors did the whole thing as if they were telecommuters," Piskurich says. "We put together files they had to share and things they had to do. It all revolved

The more closely a training program can approximate a telecommuting experience, the better.

around the processes of telecommuting — sharing what your ten greatest fears are, a file on how to overcome problems of workaholism. We gave them a taste of what it's like to be a telecommuter. They never saw anybody else."

Grantham offers a caveat to this approach, though. "I don't think people can be trained to be teleworkers on the Internet," he says. "It needs to be a face-to-face, interactive environment."

Your approach must be tailored to the specific needs of your business. You may find that some combination of face-to-face instruction with the opportunity to work alone in an environment that simulates what the telecommuter will face in his or her home is optimum.

2. Supervisor/Manager Training

Your telecommuting program will fall apart very quickly if you train only the telecommuters and not their managers. You will not only have to be concerned with implementing a revised management structure and approach for people who manage telecommuters. Your first challenge will be to overcome the prevailing attitudes and fears that your managers may have toward telecommuting.

2.1 An unnerving transition for managers

The resistance of supervisors and managers is a common barrier to implementing a successful telecommuting program, and one that must be tackled head-on at an early stage in the process.

"Very often, supervisors are afraid of telecommuting," says George Piskurich. "They think it's going to put them out of business." But in reality, Piskurich points out, "if you have a lot of telecommuters, you need even better supervisory skills."

In an employment environment marked by downsizing and a continuing emphasis on cost-cutting, this fear is understandable. It is this fear, Dr. Grantham believes, that is at the basis of most managers' hesitance to embrace the concept of telecommuting. "The typical 'If I can't see them, how do I know they're working?' attitude really is a red herring, I believe. What I've found at the core of the concern for managers really turns out to be their uncertainty, or concern that they won't be valued by the company if they're managing teleworkers." Grantham tells of a manager who once told him that the boss came out of his office, looked at all of the empty cubicles and said, "What do I need you for?" This, Grantham believes, really gets at the heart of the hesitation that many managers feel.

Dr. Grantham points out that managers may have concerns about being undervalued if they were to manage teleworkers.

A certain anxiety regarding management technique can crop up as well. This is where a solid training program is most vital for managers. Learning to make the transition from managing time to managing projects is a critical shift for most managers. "One of the key challenges for managers," says Roger Herman, strategic business futurist, CEO of the Herman Group in Greensboro, and author of *Keeping Good People*, "is the shift from activity-based management to results-based management. You're not going to know if that person's sitting at their desk at 8:00 a.m., or how many brcaks thcy'rc taking." In a telecommuting relationship, time is not the most important factor.

These are major shifts in the traditional approach to managing. How do you manage people you can't see? How do you measure performance if not by hours worked?

2.2 A structure for supervisory training

"I think managers often believe that they know more about managing and are more competent at it than they really are," says Gil Gordon. "This has been the curse of every training person to walk the face of the earth. How do you stimulate some interest without wanting to intimidate or browbeat them?" Gordon approaches this issue by —

- Teaching managers that "everything they have been doing so far is not wrong and that there is not some brand new theory of management that must be adopted where they have to learn all new jargon and so on."
- Focusing on the basics. "The essence of training for the manager is to stay focused on those good, old-fashioned Management 101 topics that managers have always been talked to about, but that most managers get away from doing because they have the luxury of frequent close contact in the office."

"My approach for the training," says Gordon, "is mostly a matter of fine-tuning what we hope they're already doing and maybe introducing some new concepts, as opposed to starting from scratch, which is not necessary and which will not gain many fans."

The message is keep it simple. You don't need to create chaos among your managers. You simply need to look at the telecommuter-manager relationship and address the basic issues. As Roger Herman points out, even training on such simple skills as how to communicate effectively over the phone or by e-mail can have a positive impact on the relationship. "One of the things the supervisor has to be sensitive to, of course, is maintaining that high level of communication, keeping them involved and realizing that managing someone you can't see is considerably different than walking around the cubicle wall to see that they're there at 8:00 in the morning."

An important part of this process, then, is recognizing exactly what about the telecommuter-manager relationship will need to be addressed. Many of these details will inevitably arise as you are working toward implementing your program, but it is a good idea to have a planned period of observation and assessment before you begin.

Bernadette Fusaro provides a service to managers called process consultation. "We will go into an area and identify for the manager ahead of time what the barriers will be to implementing flexibility," she says. "We look at the way employees communicate. We look at areas that will potentially be problems before we even introduce it to employees." This groundwork helps to alleviate concerns that managers may have and also identifies specific areas that need to be addressed as the telework arrangement is formalized.

Gil Gordon's manager training program for managers of telecommuters is a two-hour session designed to "improve the quality of the telecommuting program by taking the guesswork out of remote work, and making sure that everyone has thought through the critical issues." The following topics are covered:

- Managing by results instead of by observation
- Fine-tuning skills for setting performance standards and giving ongoing performance feedback
- Keeping telecommuters linked to the office
- Career management issues for telecommuters
- Spotting problems early and dealing with them effectively

The techniques of remote management are discussed in detail in chapter 7.

2.3 Supervisor's checklist

Telecommuters and their managers need to attend a joint training meeting in which they develop objectives and work out all the minor details in advance.

As part of the training and orientation process for managers, it can be helpful to offer some specific information on expectations for the management process, or helpful tips that can aid managers in effectively overseeing their telecommuters.

The California Department of Personnel Administration uses a "Supervisor's Checklist for Telecommuters" (reproduced here as Checklist 3) designed to start the relationship on a basis of mutual understanding and ensure that all the details of the arrangement have been covered.

3. Team Training

It's not enough to hold training sessions for telecommuters and then hold training sessions for their managers. At some point along the way, these two groups need to be brought together. "The telecommuter has to understand what the supervisor's problems are going to be, and vice versa," Piskurich points out.

At Merrill Lynch, joint sessions are used as a forum for discussion as well as an opportunity to develop objectives. "The employees bring their work objectives, and the manager and employee sit down and discuss the expectations of the arrangement," Fusaro says. "The manager will talk about when he or she expects the employee to be available and what kind of communication they will use. They iron out ahead of time how this arrangement is going to work. That's a big step because things are not left to chance."

"The joint sessions, I find the most interesting," says Gordon, "and attendees do too. It's really a negotiating and planning session." At these sessions Gordon asks telecommuters and managers to discuss such basic issues as "How many days a week are you going to telecommute?," "Which days will they be?," and "How often will you check e-mail?"

"As mundane as these questions may seem," he says, "I have seen over and over again that if they are not discussed in advance you wind up with two very different sets of expectations that are really pretty dangerous when they come up against each other."

Gordon's telecommuter training programs schedule the joint session as the final session, after the telecommuters and their managers

CHECKLIST 3
SUPERVISOR'S CHECKLIST FOR TELECOMMUTERS
(California Department of Personnel Administration)

Name of telecommuter ______________________________

Name of supervisor ______________________________

Date completed ______________________________

- ❑ Employee has read the orientation documents and the telecommuting policy.
- ❑ Employee has been provided with a schedule of core hours or guidelines for flexing work hours.
- ❑ Equipment issued is documented.
- ❑ Performance expectations have been discussed and are clearly understood. Assignments and due dates are documented.
- ❑ Requirements for adequate and safe office space at home have been reviewed with the employee and the employee certifies that those requirements have been met.
- ❑ Requirements for care of equipment assigned to the employee have been discussed and are clearly understood.
- ❑ The employee is familiar with the requirements and techniques for computer information security and has received a copy and read the Information Security Guidelines.
- ❑ Phone contact procedures have been clearly defined and unit secretaries and receptionists have received training.
- ❑ The employee has read and signed the Telecommuter's Agreement prior to actual participation in the program.

have undergone training separately. The topics covered in this joint discussion session include the following:

- Detailing the schedule, availability, phone coverage, and office days
- Planning the first few weeks of telecommuting
- Minimizing effects on department workflow
- Providing technical (equipment) support as needed
- Dealing with system shutdowns and other problems

Training for a telecommuting program should include the entire organization, not just telecommuters. All staff should be aware of how telecommuting will affect them.

4. Training the Rest of the Staff

The workforce at large also needs to have some training and education to familiarize them with the telecommuting program. "If the entire organization isn't trained and educated about telecommuting — how it's being implemented, who is being selected and why," Steve Schilling says, "then folks that aren't even involved in it can be impacted in negative ways in terms of losing touch with people in the program."

But the training challenge doesn't stop here. There's yet another important group that must be considered. Grantham stresses that executive education is another element of telecommuting preparedness. Too often, he says, "the vice presidents and other administrators will come into the telework situation, say the company supports it, and then disappear. They're not really as sensitive, I think, as they need to be to what's going on in the telework environment. They need some education, too."

In addition to up-front education, Grantham typically brings the executive staff back into the process about six months into the program, using productivity measurements as the basis for business case analysis. "We bring it back to the executives in terms of what impact it's having on productivity, cost, and customer satisfaction. That usually makes believers out of them."

5. After Training

It's important, Gordon says, to plan training sessions as close as possible to the actual time when telecommuting will begin. "I think training creates some momentum, some excitement, and it's a shame to waste that. It's like teaching somebody how to play golf and then they don't get to go out on the golf course for six months. No matter how good the training is, people either just forget it or they tend to lose that edge."

Are potential telecommuters ever discouraged from telecommuting after they go through the training process? It happens. "We had some people who, after the training, said, 'This is not for me,' " Fusaro recalls. "But it's been minimal. We've had a few people who have been home for a while and said, 'I miss the interaction.' " But, she says, for the most part, "the ones that go through the training like it, and we've had very little fallout."

6. Tips for Starting Telecommuters

Steve Schilling and Telecommute Solutions offer the following tips for telecommuters. These are concerns that should be addressed in your telecommuting training program and should become fundamental to the way in which your program operates:

- *Face time is very important.* If you are a regular telecommuter, use your day at the office for face-to-face meetings and plain old human connections. Don't be afraid to ask for meeting agendas and starting and ending times. You can nicely let people know that your time in the office is limited so you need to manage it carefully. After just a few meetings, they will realize that your time is important and will not waste it. We have found that meetings that involve telecommuters are more effective and more productive than those made up of office staffers only.
- *The biggest mistake is to hide behind e-mail or voice mail.* Staying in touch with your manager or coworkers is one of the most important things that you can do for yourself. Don't rely on days in the office to provide the human touch. By cultivating and nourishing your relationships with your coworkers, you can stay informed of important developments within the company and have friends you can call on if you need support. The fear of invisibility will not be an issue if you continue to communicate; and the responsibility to do so is yours!
- *Share knowledge and expertise.* As a telecommuter, you should add as much to the equation from a home office as from the

enterprise office. The second biggest mistake you can make is to let non-telecommuting colleagues believe that you are a casual worker. By your words and deeds, let everyone know that they should expect the same standard of work from you as from office workers.

- *Be aware of jealousy and misconceptions.* Don't brag about your lack of commuting or any other of the benefits you have discovered about telecommuting. While you don't have to lie about the benefits and rewards of telecommuting, we suggest that you tell the truth when asked but don't keep telling everyone at the office how lucky you are.

Merryl Lynch's telecommuting training process focuses on awareness, training, technology simulation, and ongoing support.

7. Case Study 1

Janice Miholics, vice president, manager of private client technology for alternative work arrangements at Merrill Lynch, Pierce, Fenner & Smith, Inc., has developed a training program that is structured around a four-step process designed to educate employees and managers about alternative approaches to the work environment while providing the tools, such as technology, to facilitate such change within the organization. The four steps are awareness, training, technology simulation lab, and ongoing support.

Anyone who has submitted a telecommuting proposal during the previous four weeks will go through a two-hour training session that may involve as many as 10 to 12 people to as few as one person, Miholics says. An unanticipated advantage of this training, she says, is the network the telecommuters form with other trainees.

"We sit down with them and go over all of the aspects of what it will be like to telecommute. We spend a lot of time asking what concerns they have." Miholics wants to find out how potential telecommuters envision the relationships, whether they've talked to their clients and coworkers, and whether they feel their manager is supportive. "Training is the best time to get those things out in the open," she says.

The training for telecommuters also focuses quite extensively on setting up the home office. "We verify two things," Miholics says. "We ask them to describe the space in which they will be working and we verify that this is not a substitute for day care. We tell them right up front that whatever child care arrangements they have in place will have to be maintained."

In addition to technical information, training covers the impact of telecommuting on the family and how to manage the expectations of the people in their lives. "It's important the family understands that when the telecommuter is working, he or she is working. It's not the neighborhood drop off for UPS. Even managing the neighbors can sometimes be critical. By bringing it out in the open and having an open discussion, there are no hidden expectations or misunderstandings," Miholics says.

This is valuable information for telecommuters. In fact, she says, one telecommuter told her that he appreciated the advice to share information about the telecommuting arrangement with his children. One of his children thought Dad must have lost his job. Why else would he be home three days a week?

Another two-hour session focuses on training for the managers of the telecommuters. Managers are given a brief overview of the ergonomic set-up requirements, and the remainder of the time is spent talking about "managing by objectives as opposed to managing by face time."

A third two-hour session brings the telecommuters together with their managers. Together, each manager and telecommuter defines what the telecommuter will be expected to do while telecommuting. Merrill Lynch, Miholics says, has a very strong performance management system. Each year objectives, deliverables, and dates are established and agreed upon by employees and managers. "We ask the managers and telecommuters to bring their objectives with them to this joint planning session, and they go through them and define the milestones. This is also where the manager and telecommuter may work out any communication schedules they feel are appropriate."

Once these sessions have been completed, the telecommuter goes into the simulation lab. "We replicate the current environment for the employee on a laptop so that, wherever they are, their location is irrelevant," Miholics says. The telecommuters will typically spend six days over a two-week period in the simulation lab where they receive technical instruction and have the opportunity to simulate the environment they will soon be working in at home. "The lab gives us an opportunity to see how comfortable the person is with the technology itself, and shows us the level of support that the person may require. It also gives us the chance to test out the hardware."

After telecommuters receive instruction, they are left alone and, for the next six days, are "pretty much doing their job." But, Miholics points out, "They're right next to my tech people. The goal is to get them acclimated to what it's like working off-site as much as possible. It also helps the telecommuter plan out what they're going to need to work from home — even the basics like a stapler or tape dispenser."

At the end of the six days, employees take a quiz from the Merrill Lynch Web site and are tested on various technical skills they learned in the lab. Then, Miholics says, "we send them home."

Miholics' team provides ongoing technical, communications, and administrative support for all telecommuters via a help line number and an e-mail support mailbox. A home inspection is performed to ensure the safety of the telecommuters while working from their homes and, on a quarterly basis, focus groups and surveys are conducted to measure the success of the program and to address any suggested areas of improvement.

8. Case Study 2

Training is mandatory for telecommuters at Arthur Andersen Performance & Learning, and "highly recommended for supervisors," says Debra Tucholski, Senior Manager. About 90 percent of the supervisors participate in the training, which covers four areas:

(1) technology training

(2) telework training

(3) supervisor training

(4) team training

Technology training is a hands-on experience in which the telecommuters bring their laptops and learn technology skills, such as how to access the network remotely from a dial-up system, how to do some basic trouble shooting, and how to optimize the software they have available to them.

In the half-day telework training session, Tucholski says, "there's a lot of opportunity for our teleworkers to ask questions of the instructor and of each other. They really get a good dialogue going." An important part of this session is "the business case — why are we doing this and what do we expect to get out of it," as well as how to stay in touch while working remotely and how to plan and manage time.

A unique aspect of the training is a focus on the AAPL telework database — a tool that has been developed to administer the telework process. The database includes the telework agreement, a resource section with pertinent information and links to helpful Internet sites, and a discussion area where telecommuters are able to share tips and experiences with other telecommuters.

Another half-day session is held just for the supervisors and is, Tucholski says, "highly discussion based." Again the business case is covered, but a great deal of the time is spent focusing on communication issues, including a topic on leading remote teams, which includes a discussion of what happens if there's a problem in the arrangement and how the supervisor should respond.

A team training session is also held to give the telecommuters and their managers an opportunity to work out the details of the arrangement. Groups are formed based on common interests — one group may be interested in communication, another in technology — and participants are provided with an opportunity to discuss and clarify concerns and develop strategies to overcome them. Team training also offers an opportunity for telecommuters and their managers to hammer out the elements of their individual agreements. "They talk about things like how they prefer to be contacted and how often and the types of meetings they are expected to come to the office for," Tucholski says.

"Altogether, our teleworkers are in about 16 hours of training — our supervisors about eight hours. I would call our training a key factor in the success of the rollout."

AAPL program evaluations at both the organizational and individual level show that both teleworkers and their supervisors are less concerned after training about issues like productivity, communication, and technology than they were before the training. In short, it works.

Chapter 7
MANAGING TELECOMMUTERS

"Developing a results-oriented system for managing performance is fundamental to successful supervision of a home worker."

— Tom Joseph
Bookminders, Inc.

Executive Summary

What if one of my employees wants to telecommute and I don't think that employee would be a good candidate?

Your decision of whether or not to allow an employee to telecommute should be based on objective criteria that are widely communicated to employees. Not every employee will be a good candidate for telecommuting, and you should not feel obligated to allow any employee to telecommute.

How can I keep track of what my telecommuting employees are doing?

The same way you should be keeping track of what any of your employees are doing. Your staff should be judged on the outcomes of their work, not on the processes used to obtain results. Work with each telecommuter to identify specific job-related expectations and objectives. Criteria might include the quantity of work output, quality of work output, and adherence to deadlines.

What will the impact on employees and customers be when I have telecommuters on my staff?

The needs of customers — both external and internal — are extremely important and should be foremost in your mind when establishing a telecommuting program. There should be either no impact, or a positive impact. If there is the potential for a negative impact, telecommuting should not be an option.

How can I deal with the social-interaction needs of telecommuters?

Isolation can be a very real issue for telecommuting staff, but there are a number of ways to help telecommuters maintain their positions as part of the work team.

Regularly scheduled days in the office, frequent communication, and scheduled events and meetings are all methods that managers and companies have used to maintain interaction and to ensure that telecommuters do not become invisible or forgotten.

What if some supervisors allow employees to telecommute and others don't?

For telecommuting to be effective, managers must be behind the effort. While some companies implement telecommuting across the organization, many leave the decision up to individual managers. Hesitant managers should be encouraged to make their decisions based on the unique requirements of the positions in their departments and the skills and capabilities of employees.

What if the telecommuting arrangement just doesn't work?

There is always the chance that the arrangement will not work out — for you or for the telecommuter. This is an issue that should be addressed in the telecommuting agreement. As with any other employee-performance situation, you should be prepared to address this issue quickly and directly if it comes up.

MANAGING TELECOMMUTERS

Even in a non-telecommuting situation, managing employees can be a challenge. Many managers become managers because of their expertise in their field, without having any formal management training and frequently learning through trial and error. It's not surprising, then, that managers often balk at allowing employees to telecommute. Managing is hard enough without the added stress and uncertainty of trying to keep track of people who aren't even in the building! As discussed in chapter 6, managers are often reluctant or wary when it comes to the topic of telecommuting. Misconceptions abound, and these misconceptions can prevent telecommuting arrangements from developing, or sabotage them once they're in place. But what managers sometimes don't realize is that telecommuting can easily become a win-win situation, improving manager-employee relations, management techniques and effectiveness, and productivity.

1. The Truth about Managing Telecommuters

AG Communication Systems (AGCS) has approximately 2,100 employees located throughout North America. Of that number, about 1,355 are registered teleworkers, which includes both full-time telecommuters and those that may work away from the office on a more casual basis. The following is from the AGCS handbook for managers of teleworkers:

Since telecommuters cannot be visually supervised, they must be evaluated on the attainment of goals.

> *The skills you have now as a coach/manager will serve you well when overseeing teleworkers. Basic management tools are just as important for teleworkers as they are for people in the office, but you may need to tailor your supervision for those working at home. "Management by Walking Around" won't work. You'll probably find that you need to focus more on results than appearance. Scheduling might get tricky. And you'll be called upon to show trust and support to employees who are teleworking — and to those who are not. Remember, it takes two to telework.*
>
> *Results are what count — not face time, putting in long hours, working "overtime," or any of the other "traditional" ways of measuring performance. [This is] much the same as any other type of management except it truly tests your skills. It requires an added level of communication, more carefully crafted and measurable objectives, and clear and direct feedback.*

One of the questions posed by interviewers who prepared the report *Moving Telecommuting Forward: An Examination of Organizational Variables* (July 1999), the result of an extensive study of twelve managers of telecommuters conducted at the National Center for Transportation and Industrial Productivity at the New Jersey Institute of Technology (NJIT), was: "How is productivity measured for telecommuters?" According to the report, the managers of telecommuters, who also managed non-telecommuters, reported in all instances that productivity measurement was similar for both. Goal achievement was mentioned most frequently, followed by work timeliness, contract and sales, work accuracy, cost efficiency, and, in one instance, publications. What is notable about all of these measures, according to the report, is that they focus on work outcomes and not on work process. It's not *how* the work gets done that matters, it's *what* gets done that counts.

2. Traits of Successful Telecommuter Managers

The traits of successful managers of telecommuters are actually no different from the traits of any successful managers — with the exception, perhaps, of a heightened need for excellence in communication, goal setting, and providing feedback.

TeleCommute Solutions, Inc. asked current managers of telecommuters to identify which attributes of management they considered most important. More than 50 percent of these managers identified adequate planning skills as a critical requirement to achieve success in this environment. The second critical skill identified by these managers was leadership. According to president Stephen Schilling, "This skill was seen as the ability to motivate, facilitate, and inspire telecommuters as effectively as if they were traditional office workers."

Clearly, the skills of planning and leadership are elements of any managerial relationship. But what other qualities must a manager of telecommuters possess? There are a number:

- *Comfort with supervising a remote workforce.* This is a threshold issue. Many managers simply cannot overcome their perceived need to keep employees in their sight.
- *Understanding what is required of the position.* The manager must clearly know the requirements of the position and be able to quantify or measure the output expected from the position.
- *Ability to clearly articulate goals and objectives.* Telecommuters must know what is expected of them. Management must be able to outline, specifically, the expectations and job standards that the telecommuter will be expected to meet.
- *Effective interpersonal communication.* Communication is key to a successful telecommuting relationship. Managers must establish means of interacting with the telecommuter, and allowing the telecommuter to interact with the rest of the staff through both face-to-face and technological methods.
- *Ability to provide clear and consistent feedback.* Managers must be willing and able to provide telecommuters with frequent and specific feedback. At any sign that the relationship is not working, or that objectives are not being met, the manager must immediately address the situation and, if necessary, rethink the approach.

To gauge managers' readiness to supervise telecommuters, Sprint offers a short assessment tool that, according to Alan Coleman, provides a useful resource both for the company and for managers. It allows

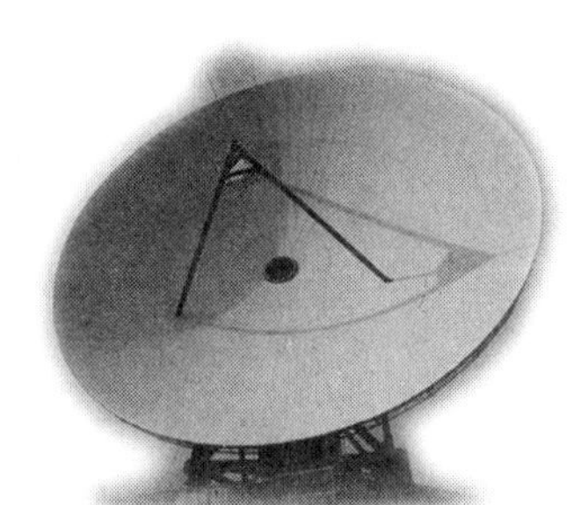

Not all managers are able to do away with visual supervision as a management technique. Alan Coleman of Sprint predicts that the structure of management will change as technology becomes more prevalent.

them to identify areas where improvements may be needed and to clearly indicate what the expectations of this role are.

The tool consists of two parts — seven questions on the first part assess the manager's general management skills; nine questions on the second part assess, specifically, the skills the manager has that would be applicable to managing telecommuters. Questions are true/false and consist of statements such as "I usually hold a staff meeting with all employees two times a month or less," "I rely on voice mail and e-mail to consult with my employees," and "I regularly hold impromptu meetings." Managers rate each statement on a scale of 1 to 6, on which 1 is "not at all true" and 6 is "completely true." Managers whose responses are all 5 or higher fall into the group that is seen as having high potential to manage telecommuters. Those who score in the 3 to 4 range have potential but need to make some minor adjustments in their management style. A tool such as this one may make a world of difference in your telecommuting program, especially during the start-up and/or transition stages.

As we have seen, the skills required to manage telecommuters are comparable to the skills required when supervising any employees. Yet managers of telecommuters need to fine-tune, and perhaps at times re-think, their managerial approaches.

3. Setting Objectives

Telecommuter performance must be measured on the attainment of established goals, and this affects a manager's approach to setting objectives.

Tom Joseph owns Bookminders, Inc., a business that provides accounting services to 150 clients through a network of 40 employees who work in various geographic locations — out of their homes. He says that "developing a results-oriented system for managing performance is fundamental to successful supervision of a home worker." Each employee's assignments are designed to focus on deliverables. Customers, he says, "are the most important source for determining quality." Therefore, customer satisfaction is monitored regularly through reviews that provide objective insight into both individual and company performance. In addition, Bookminders has invested in software systems that allow employees to track their time and monitor their productivity. Each month this information is gathered electronically for all employees and "analyzed to help us spot situations where training or changes to our systems will improve the overall quality of our service."

Managers must set and articulate clear goals, making sure that both they and the telecommuters understand what is expected. In addition, more frequent evaluation may be necessary where performance, goals, and expectations can be discussed along with a thorough evaluation of any signs of problems or emerging issues.

To develop job standards, identify the most important areas of responsibility for the position. Next, develop measurable standards for these areas.

Stephen Schilling of TCS emphasizes the need for specificity of performance objectives. "Break up the objectives into manageable chunks," he advises, "and be sure to negotiate time frames for completion of each project when applicable. Before you can review objectives, they should be clearly defined, with measurable output such as completed reports or written codes. These can be measured in quantity, quality, and time-to-complete."

Carol Stein of HR Library agrees with the necessity for clear, measurable objectives. "You can assume almost nothing," she says. "You have to be very clear and concise in what you ask for."

The process for setting objectives can be broken down into two distinct and very important areas of consideration: establishing job standards, and establishing goals.

3.1 Establishing job standards

Establishing job standards is a process that begins the moment the telecommuter is hired and continues throughout the employment relationship. It involves clear communication of expectations and standards and development of specific, measurable goals.

The job description is a good starting point for indicating what is expected, but it is just a starting point. An explanation of job standards can help indicate to employees the specific expectations for their positions. Employees also need to know the goals of their positions and how those goals tie into department and company performance.

The first step in developing job standards is to identify the critical aspects of the job. What elements of the position are necessary to keep the department and the company operating efficiently? Once the areas of responsibility have been identified, three or four standards (or key results) that represent satisfactory performance levels need to be established. It is critical that these standards be objective measures of performance. More specifically, managers can use the following measures in establishing standards:

(a) *Quality.* How many errors, omissions, or complaints will you tolerate over a given period of time?

(b) *Quantity.* How many units of production will you expect over a given period of time?

(c) *Timeliness.* Time standards can be written in terms of daily, weekly, monthly, or quarterly deadlines for task completion or amount of turnaround time permitted.

(d) *Cost efficiency.* Some positions have responsibility for meeting budgets or impacting costs. In these cases your standards might reflect a maximum dollar budget or a plus or minus variance from the stated budget.

Unfortunately, not all job tasks readily lend themselves to establishing clearly defined standards. It can be challenging to come up with quantifiable measurements for certain tasks. Your goal should be to define the most critical elements of the job and, at a minimum, to establish standards that are clear enough that you have an objective way of evaluating telecommuters' performance. For example:

JOB	TASK	STANDARD
Salesperson	Generate leads	X leads/day, week, month, etc.
	Selling product	$X/week, month, quarter, year, etc.
Accountant	Reports	Identify specific reports that are to be made available by a certain date each month, quarter, year, etc. A standard might also be developed relating to accuracy of the reports.
Computer programmer	Program development	Specify time frame from consultation to implementation based on various common programming tasks required by the organization.

3.2 Establishing goals

Well-defined goals allow both the telecommuter and manager to have a clear understanding of expectations and provide a benchmark against which to judge performance.

Goals should be —

- Specific. A goal should state "Increase sales by 20 percent," rather than simply "Increase sales."
- Mutually agreed upon.
- Difficult, yet achievable.
- Comprehensive. Goals should cover all critical areas of the telecommuter's job.

Establishing the details of goals and objectives should be the joint responsiblity of the manager and the telecommuters. Together, they should cover the following tasks:

(a) Identify objectives based on organizational and departmental goals. If a system of measurement is already in place, it should work just as well in a telecommuting environment as it does in the office.

(b) Develop schedules with assigned responsibility for specific task completion. Make it very clear who will be responsible for what and when deliverables are expected. Be sure that telecommuters know how their performance is being measured and what the standards for performance are.

(c) Set up times to determine the progress of the employees' tasks. This may be a designated point during the program, upon completion of certain tasks, or on a recurring (i.e., weekly) basis.

(d) Establish ongoing means of communicating work expectations, including due dates, quality expectations, and any other measurable criteria. This may include face-to-face meetings, electronic submission of reports, or conference calls.

It is important that the manager take the time to become familiar with the telecommuters' tasks. Managers must understand the time involved for completing tasks and the resources required to see projects

Tom Joseph, CEO of Bookminders, believes in finding ways to quantify telecommuters' work. Wages can then be based on measurable outcomes rather than hours worked.

through to completion. They must ensure that telecommuter goals are neither more nor less stringent than those set for employees doing similar work at the office. They must establish a smoothly functioning working relationship with their telecommuters, and above all, they must communicate every last detail, in detail.

Some of these details will inevitably have to be worked out along the way, as individual telecommuters, with their specific needs and situations, settle into a work routine. However, some basic considerations can be dealt with from the start. Managers should consider the following:

- Are there core hours during which you want telecommuters to be available?
- Are work hours flexible?
- How often should telecommuters call the office or check their voice mail and e-mail?
- How quickly should telecommuters return messages?
- How often should telecommuters communicate with their clients and coworkers?
- What security or confidentiality issues may be involved?

At Bookminders, Tom Joseph has established a quantitative system that he uses both to evaluate and to compensate his telecommuting staff. With a background in engineering, quantifying the process came naturally to him. Clients are billed based on deliverables, such as the number of journal entries made or the number of checks cut. "We bill our clients based on a formula and we compensate our people based on that same formula," Joseph says. "Neither I nor the client have to worry about how many hours people work." In fact, Joseph believes that "the idea of setting up a deliverables-based compensation system is really the secret to what we're doing — it's what has enabled us to grow from one employee to 40 and to have 200 clients." Can this same process work in other organizations? Joseph thinks so. "If people could come up with a value for being able to program a certain function, or number of screens, or whatever, they could bid this work out on a per-screen or per-report basis. Telemarketers could be paid by number of calls."

4. Providing Feedback

Don't restrict performance evaluations to an annual event. Evaluation should be a continuous process.

"How am I doing?"

It is no use having established objectives if the telecommuter does not know whether or not he or she is adequately meeting them. Since telecommuters are away from the office and not part of the informal communication and feedback process that often takes place between managers and employees, it is important to establish formal channels and processes for providing feedback on performance.

Start from the premise that your telecommuters want to do a good job. Their goal is to succeed. In order to do that, they need to receive regular and specific feedback from you about how they are doing. If you are remiss in letting them know when they have or have not met or exceeded your expectations, they cannot possibly improve their performance.

Establish a regular schedule for review and feedback. Evaluation should be directly tied to the job standards and goals that you have already established with the telecommuter. When creating your review schedule, ensure that:

- Employees understand the process that will be used to review their performance. Explain how the review process will work, what criteria they will be measured on, and how frequently you will communicate with them about their performance.
- Feedback is provided regularly throughout the year — not just at the formal annual review.
- You are constructively candid. Be direct, but make sure that your constructive feedback is focused on objective job criteria, not personal characteristics or traits of the employee.
- Feedback is two-way. To maximize your relationship with your telecommuting staff, you will need feedback from them as well.
- The time you're able to spend with your remote employee may be limited, so be sure to make the most of it. Reinforce positive behaviors and respond to unsatisfactory performance immediately. Take advantage of all communication tools available to you to provide employees with timely and ongoing feedback.

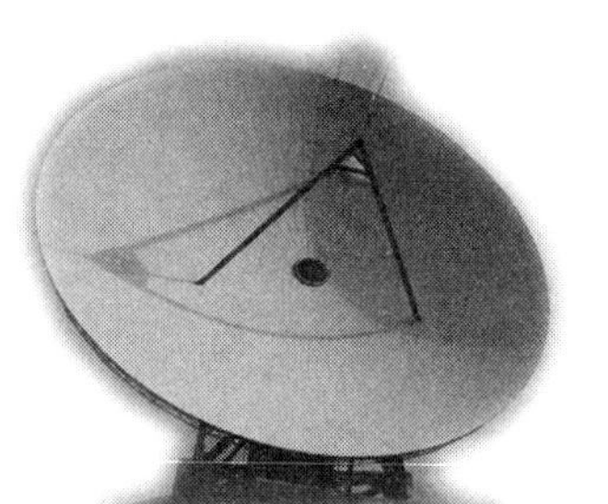

Don't assume that all telecommuters communicate the same way. You should be flexible enough to adjust to the communication needs of each telecommuter.

5. Communication

Communication is of the utmost importance in a telecommuter-manager relationship. It is key to the success of the program. This cannot be stressed enough.

Putting efficient communication systems in place is your first major step as a manager of telecommuters, but it doesn't end there. The system must be easy to use, probably modified for certain individual telecommuter needs, and continually updated and improved as problems or new strategies arise. Both telecommuter and manager must be vigilant in their adherence to the systems of communication.

In Canada, KPMG surveyed 1,600 large- and medium-sized companies in the private sector and 425 organizations in the public sector. The survey showed that a wide range of tactics are used in order to retain a sense of community between the organization and the telecommuter. Ninety-one percent of employers require telecommuters to come into the office weekly or on demand. E-mail, teleconferencing, and written materials are also employed to keep the telecommuter connected with the on-site staff and current on organization issues. In addition to standard office equipment, the majority of employers supply communication devices such as cell phones, pagers, telephones, and modems.

"I have seven telecommuters in my group," says Janice Miholics of Merrill Lynch, "and I have a different way of working with each one of them because each one has a different style and each one has different needs. One likes a very defined structure. She says, 'I would like you to know that I'm checking my e-mails at 9:30, at 11:00, and at 1:30.' With another telecommuter, I have 15-minute conference calls. And with another, unless something happens during the day that means we need to have contact, we just talk at the end of the day because that's what works best for us." What's important, Miholics says, "is for the telecommuter and the manager to find a way that makes them most comfortable."

To be most effective at communicating with telecommuting staff, take a cue from Miholics: find out the communication preferences of each of your telecommuters and be flexible in your interactions with them. Using only one system or schedule will not be an effective communication approach. As Miholics and others have discovered, telecommuters' communication needs vary widely. Your goal is to develop interactions that work most effectively for all involved, and to ensure that telecommuters can meet their goals and be productive.

5.1 The technology of communication

"Today, collaboration is the cornerstone of business," says Jim Miller, general manager of US West Extended Workplace Solutions. "From my experience as both a remote team member and a team leader, technology can create the collaborative virtual space, but it takes more than high-tech tools to create an effective collaborative environment. It takes new ways of working with each other and using the appropriate technology tools to be able to communicate and let the distance disappear."

Miller says that the right technology tools can keep team members productive wherever their work takes them. His team uses—

(a) Collaboration software tools, such as NetMeeting. "This enables us to share (and even co-author) documents, thus reducing the number of drafts that we need to fax or e-mail and maintaining version control."

(b) Speakerphones. "But only," he says, "if we don't sound like we're speaking from a cave." Miller recommends investing in good-quality speakerphones or, even better, headsets.

(c) A team "white space." "We have a place on our intranet where my team can post messages, documents, calendars, databases, and any frequently requested information such as lists, presentations, or even recommendations on hotels for the road warriors."

(d) Voice or video conferencing tools. "Sometimes we use the simple three-way calling feature and other times we use a voice conference bridge. We've even used video conferencing to review rough cuts of a video." The most cost-effective options, Miller says, "will vary depending on the number of participants and the goals of your virtual meeting."

Technology can help to maintain communication with distant team members, but, Miller advises, it's important to establish some guidelines and rules. For example:

(a) Be prepared. It's a waste of your teammates' time if you haven't looked at the agenda, read the materials, and thought about the topic at hand before the virtual meeting. Ask to reschedule if necessary.

(b) Make your presence known. If a person new to the group joins a call, then throughout the duration of the meeting, everyone should identify himself or herself before speaking. If you must join the call late, announce your presence — no lurking!

(c) Keep extraneous noise to a minimum. Shuffling papers and side conversations are distracting and can even drown the main thread of conversation. (One way to control noise is to use the mute button until you speak.)

(d) Do not multi-task. For a set period of time, devote your full attention to the team. Believe me, they can tell if you don't!

(e) Avoid "stepping on someone's line." Actors learn not to talk on top of each other so everyone can be heard. The same rule applies to conference calls.

(f) Use active listening skills. If you're in a voice conference, you do not have the advantage of "listening" to body language, and need to try harder to fully hear what the person may or may not be saying. Use rephrasing techniques to be sure, instead of assuming.

(g) Encourage participation. If you're the team leader, make sure all team members voice their opinions. The shy ones may need extra time and encouragement to participate.

Stephen Schilling of TeleCommute Solutions offers the following tips to enhance virtual communication:

- Establish regular, mutually agreed-upon communication times. Telephone calls, teleconferences, videoconferences, and chat areas can all be entered at an agreed-upon time.
- Make certain that off-site workers understand their worth to the organization. Devise methods to make these workers feel included in the team spirit. For example, have good-natured team contests or virtual coffee breaks.
- Have social events periodically where all workers can meet in person.
- Circulate an online newsletter to keep everyone abreast of projects, discoveries, innovations, and even errors. Solicit contributions from all team members.

- If your workers are regionalized, appoint one of the workers to be the initiator of communication and social activities. Groups that meet informally to share values or special interests can be effective.
- If in-person meetings are out of the question at a particular time, do your best to hold a videoconference. Visual communication enhances verbal communication.
- If team members are within convenient driving (or flying) distance, it's still a great idea to have weekly meetings at most or monthly meetings at least. There is no replacement for in-person sessions. Team meetings might also be held in various home-office environments to legitimize the workplace of the telecommuter.
- If workers are job sharing, have a formal handoff procedure, as well as the technology for informal communication for special situations and questions.
- Constantly research and implement state-of-the-art technology for (maintaining) productive communication.

6. Maintaining Involvement

One of the greatest fears that telecommuters have is that they will become invisible. They worry about being out of touch and overlooked for key assignments and promotions. As a manager, you should be aware of this concern and take steps to ensure that telecommuters maintain their involvement and visibility within the organization. There are a number of ways in which you can do this:

- Be honest about the changes that will occur when an employee becomes a telecommuter. Obviously, relationships will change. Address the issue head on and help the telecommuter work through his or her concerns.
- Emphasize to the telecommuter the role that he or she plays in maintaining visibility. Encourage telecommuters to take advantage of all communication tools available to them and stress the importance of establishing frequent and effective communication links to the head office.

- Provide support staff and other staff members with the home phone numbers and e-mail addresses of telecommuters so they won't be left out of general office communications.
- Keep in touch with telecommuters and provide frequent updates about what's happening back at the head office. Consider e-mail newsletters that can provide regular reports on news and events.
- Don't overlook off-site employees when selecting members for team projects, tasks, or promotions.
- Schedule regular and frequent trips to the office so telecommuters have the opportunity to interact with other members of the staff.
- Include team-building activities at regular meetings.
- Schedule frequent evaluation sessions.
- Be flexible and willing to change your style of communication or consider unique modes of interaction based on the needs of individual telecommuters.
- Make sure that telecommuters are offered the same professional growth opportunities as the rest of the staff. Some ways of doing this might include:
    - Allowing telecommuters to join professional organizations related to their current jobs or jobs they are interested in.
    - Sending telecommuters to courses to enhance their skills or help them develop additional skills.
    - Working with telecommuters on career advancement within the organization.
    - Recommending telecommuters for task forces and committees.

In a study conducted by the Georgetown University School of Business for Bell Atlantic, telecommuters at several companies — including American Express, Marriott International, and Fannie Mae — were interviewed over a period of several months. Common disadvantages that were pointed out included the fear of being left out of communication, the manager being difficult to reach when the telecommuter had a problem, and the available technologies not being compatible with their needs.

Companies have found ways to address the common pitfalls of telecommuting, however. American Express, for example, assigns telecommuters a "buddy" in the home office to be sure they are informed. Telecommuters are encouraged to spend time during work hours talking with their buddies about work-related issues to keep abreast of office developments and boost morale. Recommendations based on the Georgetown survey included training and improved communication, which have been discussed at length, and also a redefinition of authority. The survey suggests that successful telecommuting demands that workers move away from the traditional management paradigm towards a more interdependent balance of power.

7. Motivating Telecommuters

The strategies and techniques necessary to motivate telecommuters are the same as those you should already be using with your on-site employees. The following are some strategies that will work with employees both on-site and off-site:

- *Listen to your telecommuters' concerns.* Make sure that you are sincere in listening to your telecommuters and that you give fair and honest consideration to their questions and concerns.
- *Be available.* Make sure that your telecommuting employees have ready access to you by phone, e-mail, or in person.
- *Share information.* Telecommuters have a heightened need to feel included. When you share information with them, they will feel more involved in what's happening at the company. This can be as simple as letting them know about an employee's going-away party or as involved as reviewing information about the organization's strategic plan.
- *Give ample recognition for a job well done.* Provide telecommuters with frequent feedback about how they're doing and make sure that you share their accomplishments and achievements with on-site staff.
- *Provide opportunities for professional growth.* As previously discussed, telecommuters, like any employees, need to be motivated by the opportunity for growth.

If the telecommuting arrangement isn't working out, take action as soon as possible. Ignoring minor problems will lead to major problems in the future.

- *Treat telecommuters as individuals.* It is rare to find two individuals who have the same skills or personal objectives. While one telecommuter may react favorably to infrequent contact and open-ended expectations, another may require frequent visits to the office and very clear and specific direction. Take the time to get to know your telecommuters and to understand their individual goals and objectives.
- *Be open to new ideas.* Employee feedback is important to any company's success. Listen carefully to every idea presented and give each fair consideration. If you decide to use an idea, make sure that you give credit to the individual who made the suggestion.
- *Have fun!* All work and no play can make all of us dull. When employees have been working nonstop for a period of time, they need and appreciate a little time off. Allow some breaks and take time to celebrate successes. There are many ways to show your appreciation to employees. Be creative.

8. If the Relationship Doesn't Work

Not every telecommuting relationship will be a successful one. Sometimes the telecommuter decides that he or she misses the interaction and security of the traditional office setting. Or you may decide that productivity or service to customers is suffering from the telecommuting arrangement. In either case, it is important to act quickly to remedy the situation.

Unresolved issues can have a negative impact in a number of ways. There may be direct monetary cost to the organization. There may be productivity costs. There will almost certainly be morale problems, especially if you fail to take action. Other employees will quickly become frustrated if telecommuters are not pulling their weight.

A common mistake made by managers is to wait to see if the issue will resolve itself. Few people welcome conflict, and — at least initially — it appears far easier to avoid conflict than to confront it. In fact, avoiding a problem may actually result in greater frustration, effort, and cost to the organization at a later date.

If a problem surfaces, address it immediately. Just as when addressing performance issues with on-site employees, your feedback should be immediate, predictable, impersonal, and consistent. Approach the employee as soon as the issue has been noticed or reported. Selecting the appropriate tool to communicate with the employee is very important. While a minor issue (a reminder to turn in a report, for example) may be handled via e-mail, other more critical issues (i.e., a customer complaint about lack of availability) may require a face-to-face meeting. Make sure that you don't use technology as a means of avoiding an uncomfortable situation.

One of the most pervasive problems that managers have — whether managing on-site staff or telecommuters — is failure to document thoroughly. Be meticulous in your documentation.

Your comments should remain focused on the task and the objective measures of performance you have established, not on the personal habits or characteristics of the employee. Do not criticize a telecommuter for something that an employee in a comparable position at the workplace would not be criticized for. The telecommuting agreement can provide a good frame of reference and guide for addressing problems in the relationship (see chapter 3).

Finally, don't treat the employee as an adversary. Address the issue without lecturing, nagging, or losing your temper. Make sure to allow the employee an opportunity to tell his or her side of the story, and be sure to listen with an open mind.

If a problem arises, you will have to discuss the situation with the telecommuter. During this discussion, you should —

- have notes and make use of them,
- explain the facts as completely as possible,
- ask the telecommuter for his or her perspective,
- expect and allow some emotional venting,
- be specific about the consequences of continued problems, and
- provide a system for follow-up.

If the situation progresses or becomes worse, it may be necessary to either terminate the telecommuting relationship or terminate the employment relationship. In either case, it is important that you have documented the issues that have led to your decision and that you address the problem immediately and objectively.

When a performance-related incident occurs, record the date it happened, what specifically occurred, and the interaction you had with the employee. Make certain that you have informed the employee of each infraction that occurred and that you have clearly indicated what would happen if future occurrences took place.

Your goal in dealing with performance issues is not to move quickly to terminate the telecommuting or employment relationship, but to maintain a productive and effective employee. In providing the employee with information about behaviors or actions that are inconsistent with policy or expectations, you should also provide coaching and assistance in improving employee behavior. Perhaps more training is required. Perhaps the tools available to the employee are insufficient to perform the job effectively. However, do not hesitate to terminate the telecommuting arrangement if it is not meeting the needs of the department or the organization.

9. Additional Tips for Managers of Telecommuters

The telecommuter-manager relationship is an evolving one. It will be continually fine-tuned to suit the changing needs of the business, the individual needs of the telecommuter, and the professional growth of the manager. Always seek advice and examples from other managers and also from telecommuters, whether they are working for you or not.

Remember that a trusting relationship is critical. Try not to over-manage your telecommuters, making them feel as though they are under constant surveillance. Be careful, though, to find a balance between over-managing and ignoring teleworkers. Try not to become too much of an absentee manager. Maintaining the right amount of contact with your telecommuters will allow them to feel involved without feeling stifled.

You are bound to face some challenges in your telecommuting relationships, particularly if the process is new to you and/or your organization. Good organization and communication skills are your best combative measures. Help your telecommuters organize their work. Don't expect perfection, and don't expect everyone to be successful. Some employees adjust more readily to a telecommuting environment than others. Telecommuting may not work for everyone. When it doesn't, take immediate steps to develop a more workable solution.

See sample 4 for more tips from AG Communication Systems, and sample 5 for tips from the University of Houston.

SAMPLE 4
TELEWORKING ISSUES
(AG Communication Systems Telework Handbook)

Before your employees begin working at home, you might keep in mind some of these issues that can be sensitive to both teleworkers and non-teleworkers.

Suggestions for Managing Non-Teleworkers in a Teleworking Environment

Selection

As you select participants in the teleworking program, you need to work carefully with non-teleworkers to avoid their feeling "left out." Prepare in advance the necessary documentation to support your decision of who was chosen to telework. Should you have non-teleworking employees who have been excluded from the program because of poor job performance, you might begin a program to assist those employees in raising their job performance level.

Team Effort

Non-teleworkers are as critical to the program's effectiveness as the teleworkers. The success of your group depends on the efforts of everyone. Understanding the components of what makes your team successful will guarantee continued success.

Team Support

Non-teleworkers shouldn't be expected to do extra work in the office while teleworkers are working at home. Try to make sure you're consistent in assigning and providing support to your employees.

Communications Links

Establish guidelines for contacting teleworkers when an issue arises in the office that requires immediate action. Don't expect non-teleworkers to work on their own assignments as well as handling problems for teleworkers. Establish guidelines for answering the teleworkers' phones while they are teleworking. Refrain from advising callers, "Bobby is at home today." Instead, say "Bobby is unavailable at this time. I'll be happy to have her return your call as soon as she is able." Or, "You can reach Bobby at (phone number)." Additionally, have teleworkers call the office at regular intervals, and provide support staff with home phone numbers.

Contingency Plans

Establish Murphy's Law strategies to guide your workgroup through "what if" situations. Address all issues that are pertinent to the team and encourage participation from the entire team.

Sample 4 — Continued

What Happens If It's Not Working?

You and your teleworkers must understand that not everyone who tries teleworking is successful. Some reasons why the teleworker may need to end his/her participation in the program are:

Uncontrollable distractions — The neighbors and family just don't understand that while the employee is at home, they are unavailable for other activities.

Cabin fever — Being at home 24 hours a day becomes unacceptable.

Productivity and quality of work — The employee's productivity and/or the quality of the employee's work has declined since the employee has been participating in the teleworking program.

Desire or need to be around people — The employee discovers that the need for social interaction is a critical factor in his or her life.

If it becomes apparent that the employee must end his or her participation in the project, don't hold a grudge against that employee because he or she was not successful in his or her efforts. Help the employee to understand that he or she is of value to the organization and bring him or her back into the office as quickly as possible.

SAMPLE 5
MANAGING TELECOMMUTERS: TIPS FOR SUPERVISORS
(University of Houston, Health Science Center)

The University of Houston's Health Science Center offers advice on managing telecommuters:

- Managing telecommuters is not unlike managing employees on-site. It requires management skills such as goal setting, assessing progress, giving regular feedback, and managing based on outcomes. Some managers prefer dividing objectives into smaller parts and reviewing work more frequently — at least initially — to ensure the telecommuter is on track.

- Focus on quality of work, not necessarily quantity of time spent off-site.

- Identify and discuss problem areas as soon as possible and develop a plan of action to avoid bigger problems down the road.

- Be flexible enough to make changes when and where necessary.

- Include telecommuters in all appropriate office meetings, both official and social, to prevent telecommuters from feeling isolated from the office team.

- Review sections on selecting telecommuters and creating a safe/efficient work site in the Telecommuting guide to assist in managing telecommuters in your area.

- Remember that use of telecommuting is first and foremost a supervisor's option and should be reviewed/approved with careful consideration of the missions of your department and the University.

- While telecommuting can sometimes look like a benefit only to employees, most studies show that, based on benefits from such things as decreased employee turnover and increased employee productivity, a company can save several thousand dollars a year per telecommuter.

- Supervisors should give telecommuters at least 24 hours notice if they plan to visit the alternate work site to check on University equipment, the work environment, etc.

10. Case Study

At Johnson & Company, a virtual public relations and marketing firm, owner Jennifer Johnson feels she has found the right mix of people, tools, and processes to manage telecommuting relationships effectively.

The technical part is easy, she says, "but you still need to develop standards and carefully evaluate technologies." Employees are trained remotely on both the process and technology issues of their jobs. Technology is considered "a way of life." Johnson admits, though, that "we find great differences in individuals' technical understanding. Trying to find common ground is hard sometimes."

Johnson & Johnson has an online version of an orientation packet that can also be found on the company's Internet service. "We call it the e-room," she says. "People can go there and access those materials any time they want."

The processes that Johnson & Company have established allow employees to do a lot of self-monitoring and evaluation. "People, in great part, set their own rates for what's billable to a client," Johnson says. "The way they are able to increase their rate is through acquiring new experiences and abilities." Johnson & Company tracks the different skills that associates have and, Johnson says, "I challenge them to acquire new abilities." One associate recently increased her value by 25 percent by taking on a new project and successfully completing it.

Peer evaluation is also an important part of the process. "We do debriefings on projects," Johnson says, "and we've created a model for determining what we consider to be superior performance. We evaluate ourselves as a team."

Communication is a critical aspect of managing any telecommuting relationship, Johnson believes — or, in reality, of managing any relationship. Associates stay in contact in a number of ways, including e-mail, voice mail, and use of the corporate "e-room." Frequent phone conferences help team members stay in contact with each other — and with clients.

The company also meets, in person, about once each quarter. "We use these meetings as a chance to not only connect socially," Johnson says, "but also to do training." The quarterly meetings allow an opportunity to learn about new technology and to review best practices.

Johnson also brings in outside speakers to address the group. Meetings are held for three days and, Johnson says, "I put a lot of money into this — about $50,000 a year."

All employees need recognition and encouragement to stay motivated. Virtual employees are no exception. "Something we think is really important," Johnson says, "is what we call the virtual high-five. We understand that teams need to find ways of having a culture and unity beyond just getting the work done, and we look for fun ways to do this."

One year, as part of the holiday celebration, Johnson purchased silk pajamas, with the company's logo, for each associate. "I sent out the packages and wrote on the note, 'Please don't open until instructed.'" Then, during one of the team teleconference meetings, Johnson instructed the group to find their boxes and, she says, "we had a virtual rip-fest." It's a small point, she says, "but that's what it's all about."

Chapter 8
PROGRAM OUTCOMES

"It is important to learn from the research and be informed of the consequences telecommuting might have — both positive and negative — on the organization and on the employees."

— THERESA PITMAN
President, Pitman Technology Group Inc.

Executive Summary

How will I know if the program is successful?

That's really up to you. Developing some process for measuring the effectiveness of your telecommuting program is essential. In fact, you may have several different types of measurements in place, depending on the type and number of telecommuting relationships your organization has. Measurement should be based on the objectives you establish for the program and may incorporate both qualitative and quantitative measures. For instance, you may rely on verbal reports from telecommuters and their managers, surveys, or quantitative productivity measures.

What if the program is operating according to the company guidelines, but is still not working?

If your telecommuting program is still relatively new, you may have to accommodate a learning-curve period. But this is a time for revision and fine tuning. Collect whatever results are available, and discuss methods of improvement with telecommuters, their managers, and other staff.

Why do telecommuting programs fail?

There are a variety of reasons why telecommuting programs fail. Chief among these, however, are poorly defined objectives (not knowing what you wanted to achieve from the program in the first place), selecting the wrong individual or the wrong job for telecommuting, poorly conceived or nonexistent guidelines, and lack of communication.

PROGRAM OUTCOMES

Properly implemented and conscientiously managed, your telecommuting program should prove highly beneficial to both the business and its employees. When the operation is running smoothly, workers should be more productive, overhead costs should be reduced, and employee retainment should show improvement. The overall success (or failure) of the program should be as rigorously monitored as the fine details of its operations.

1. Measuring Program Outcomes

It's important to establish methods of evaluating your telecommuting program as well as the morale of both telecommuters and on-site staff. This can be done by measuring output, by surveying those involved in the program, and through direct observation. Technology also affords the means to evaluate program outcomes by measuring how many employees use remote access, for instance, or keeping track of how long online sessions last, when employees are logging in, and how frequently they connect.

The overall success (or failure) of the program should be as rigorously monitored as the fine details of its operations.

The process of evaluating your telecommuting program should be built in from the outset. Both qualitative and quantitative information

Jim Miller of US West Extended Workplace Solutions advises companies to decide exactly what they hope to gain from a telecommuting program before trying to settle the minor details.

can be used to assess the program. The criteria you select for your assessment should be based on the objectives you initially established for the program. For example, if your primary objective in starting a telecommuting program was to improve employee morale and reduce turnover, you might include a qualitative measurement of morale — perhaps self-reports from the telecommuters and other staff members — as well as quantitative measures of turnover. If your primary objective was to reduce office space costs, again, you should be able to apply quantitative measures of costs based on a before-and-after comparison.

Depending on your objectives and the measures of success you've selected, there are a variety of sources from which to obtain information. These sources may include individuals — for instance, telecommuters, telecommuter managers, non-telecommuting employees, and customers. Sources may also include data, such as turnover data, office-supply expense data, and productivity records.

Feedback to the participants in the program is very important. Share the results of whatever you're measuring and involve telecommuters (and their on-site colleagues) in any discussions on how to improve results.

2. Why Telecommuting Programs Fail

Do telecommuting programs really deliver the results that companies expect? According to Marc J. Wallace, Jr., PhD, a founding partner of the Center for Workplace Effectiveness, Inc., in Northbrook, Illinois, and co-author of *Work & Rewards in the Virtual Workplace: A "New Deal" for Organizations & Employees* (AMACOM, 1998) — no.

"Our research experience has been that telecommuting, so far, has been a disappointment for most organizations that have tried it," says Wallace. He points to four major downfalls, or problem areas, that tend to emerge over time:

(1) Lack of quality face time with people, particularly where high interaction is required by the work process or the nature of the work itself. "When I'm attached by the umbilical cord of the modem or other electronic medium, I don't have the full advantage of body language, of multiple channels of communication and the very real, but difficult to measure, intangible of human interaction."

(2) Absence from the workplace. "Unless the telecommuter is extremely sophisticated in terms of coordinating, handing things off, and leaving instructions, it can lead to a less — rather than more — productive environment."

(3) Lost creativity. "The inventiveness and energy behind innovation can get lost when people aren't interacting with each other on a regular basis. A lot of things that were good ideas get lost and are never brought to fruition because there isn't this opportunity that often presents itself in working teams to get creative and to brainstorm."

(4) Unmet expectations. "There is an assumption in telecommuting that, somehow, home is going to be a friendly, easier, quieter place to work than the office. The normal life that goes on at home can become more of a distraction — not less of a distraction."

These points, Wallace says, should be the basis of any telecommuting training program. "I believe that it's necessary, if one is going to institute telecommuting, that one take those four circumstances into account and train for them."

As we have seen in this book, there are a number of reasons why telecommuting programs may fail; but we have also seen that with appropriate methods of program implementation and management, there are many more reasons why telecommuting should succeed.

In *Moving Telecommuting Forward: An Examination of Organizational Variables,* a report based on research conducted at the National Center for Transportation and Industrial Productivity at the New Jersey Institute of Technology (NJIT), a number of recommendations were made to improve the effectiveness of telecommuting, including the following:

(a) *Readiness.* To assess the readiness of your organization for telecommuting, conduct an audit to find out how much casual telecommuting already exists. Your organization may be further ahead than you think.

(b) *Communication.* Assess the extent to which your organization is using e-mail, phone conferences, and other asynchronous forms of communication. The greater variety in telecommunication modalities used, the more readily the organization can adapt to telecommuting.

(c) *Management.* Part-time telecommuting does not appear to require much change in management style or process. Reassure managers regarding the limited requirements for change. The fact that these managers perceived virtually no change in their behaviors toward part-time telecommuters in comparison to non-telecommuters suggests that future studies should focus on full-time telecommuting arrangements. This project will continue to add managers to the database already developed.

(d) *Learning Curve.* Where full-time telecommuting is contemplated, managers and employees need to go through a learning curve as they adjust to a new working arrangement. Both should be prepared to give added effort in communication while the manager adapts to not having the employee readily available. Both need to go through some orientation to telecommuting issues. There are several sources and Web sites that are helpful in giving guidelines for successful telecommuting programs.

(e) *Equity.* The problem here involves opportunities for promotion while telecommuting full-time for an extended duration. While there may be some positions available, in most large organizations this currently does not seem to be a viable alternative. Career counseling should alert employees to maintain visibility. If long-term, full-time telecommuting is a job requirement for an employee, the employee needs to be counseled about ramifications for career progress. One alternative is to seek an organization that is comfortable with telecommuting as a full-time work arrangement. As an example, the CEO of one of the organizations sampled liked telecommuting. Such an organization would accommodate someone who has needs for long-term, full-time telecommuting.

(f) *Selection.* Currently, telecommuting is available at a professional level in the organizations sampled, but not to hourly workers. Those wishing to telecommute can select it as an option, but most organizations are not promoting it. This lack of promotion may give the impression that it is a second-class work arrangement. If an organization gives the option, then it should publicize the option as an alternative work arrangement through its Human Resource Department or equivalent.

(g) *Teamwork.* This way of assigning tasks is disrupted less by telecommuting than one might think. Teamwork while telecommuting places a priority on organizational skills and attention to detail so that participants in teleconferences have available all materials that one would normally have available at a meeting. With e-mail and fax, this should present little difficulty beyond that of getting material out before the meeting begins (as opposed to bringing material to a meeting). Coordination for a teleconference requires efforts similar to coordinating times for a face-to-face meeting. The additional element to deal with is the technology of the phone conference. Communication in between can be handled by e-mail. With distribution lists, e-mail is often a better manager of communication than the team leader, who may forget to relay messages to everyone, may relay incomplete messages, or may distort or delay relaying messages.

(h) *Moving towards remote management.* An interesting and unexpected trend discerned in this project is the move toward remote management regardless of whether employees are telecommuting or not. That is, work is becoming distributed over wider geographical areas, and managers are more and more likely to be based at locations that are apart from their subordinates. This portends a change so that managers, in general, will need the same skill set and style found among managers of telecommuters. These skills place a priority on organization, communication over a variety of modalities, an ability to set specific and unambiguous goals with employees, and the capacity to build trust of subordinates based on their performance.

Creating a successful telecommuting program requires careful attention to detail, flexibility in responding to unique personal and departmental needs, clear objectives, and identified methods of monitoring and measuring the success of telecommuting efforts and the program as a whole. The specifics of the program will vary by company and by position, but these general needs remain consistent across all programs.

3. Case Study

Theresa Pittman is the President of Pittman Technology Group Inc., a "facilitated-learning consulting firm" based in Shoal Harbour, Newfoundland. She has maintained a home office for many years, even

Theresa Pittman says it is easier to manage the work than to manage the individual.

while working in the public sector. "I found I was often able to be productive on projects by taking some time to work at home without interruptions. So when I decided to start my own company, I naturally opted to have a home-based office." She feels, she says, "part of a growing trend." "Working from home is being more readily accepted as a way to work."

Managing her staff, which consists primarily of subcontractors, is "easy" because, she points out, "I am managing the work and not the individual." In addition to subcontractors, Pittman has one full-time employee who works from home. "We communicate regularly by e-mail and telephone and only meet in person every couple of weeks. I feel confident in this arrangement since I am aware of the projects he is involved in and the time required to complete the deliverables. He is really good at letting me know how he is progressing or if there are any setbacks."

Effective communication has been a key to her success — both as a telecommuter and as a manager of telecommuters. There are, she says, "two types of communication circles." They are—

(1) communication internal to the company — with employees and subcontractors; and

(2) communication external to the company, which she refers to as network communication.

Communication with employees and subcontractors, she says, can be accomplished through various methods, including e-mail, telephone conferences, and in-person meetings. Pittman seeks out individuals who are comfortable with this type of communication. "I have worked with people in the past who need a lot more personal contact, discussion, and exploration time. This is not a fault — just their own personal communication style. Since I am aware of this variable, I choose to contract people who are more comfortable working independently, who like the control that working at home can provide, and who are goal oriented. But having said all that, it is still imperative that they have above-average communication skills!"

Network communication involves contact with individuals external to a company who represent a diverse circle of contacts — "professional teleworkers, individuals, specialists, and others who can provide guidance, assistance, project leads, and referrals." Pittman feels she has been "fortunate in being able to secure this network" and, therefore, never feels "like I'm working in vacuum." She says that joining various organizations such as the Chamber of Commerce and the Telework Association of Newfoundland and Labrador have also helped to build this network.

"Although telework might appear on the surface to be easy to implement, too many organizations and people just do it without giving it due consideration and communicating on all the various elements," Pittman cautions. "It is important to learn from the research and be informed of the consequences telecommuting might have — both positive and negative — on the organization and on the employees."

Appendix 1
TELECOMMUTING PROPOSAL

Sample Telecommuting Proposal
The University of Texas—Houston Health Science Center (www.uth.tmc.edu/)

Date:

Employee's Name:

Supervisor's Name:

I, ____(name), am requesting to telecommute with my job as ______________________________(job title), beginning on ____________________(date).

Potential impact of my telecommuting on my department may include the following (e.g., impact on operations/work flow, potential advantages, potential disadvantages):

____

____

____

The schedule I would desire for telecommuting is:

____

____

My alternative work site would be:

____

A description of this work site is:

____

(e.g., a spare bedroom with door away from most family activity that is well ventilated, has good lighting, many electrical outlets, phone jack, etc.)

Equipment I would need from this department would include:

____

____

Equipment I already own and am willing to use includes:

____

____

My expectations from the department to support me in telecommuting are:

____

____

(e.g., provide 486 PC, fax, modem, telephone line, pay for insurance on equipment)

My expectations for supervision are:

____

____

(e.g., frequency, how work would be reviewed)

Check one:

- ❑ I do not have dependent care needs
- ❑ I do have dependent care needs that are met as follows:

____

____

____

I would like to review my telecommuting agreement in ____ months to determine its effectiveness on my job performance.

Thank you for your consideration.

____

Employee Name

Appendix 2
TELECOMMUTING POLICY
AG Communication Systems Sample

Telecommuting Policy

1.0 Policy

Employees who work away from AGCS and connect via telephone or computer connections are defined as teleworkers. AGCS supports teleworking as an alternative work arrangement shifting the location of work away from the main offices of AGCS and to the worker. Coaches/Managers are encouraged to give employees' teleworking requests every consideration. Teleworking and teleworkers are classified and supported dependent upon the level and frequency of teleworking to include casual, part-time, job demand, full-time, and mobile, as well as teleworkers at satellite offices.

2.0 Scope

This Policy applies to regular full-time and part-time nonunion salaried employees at all AGCS locations, and provides guidelines to employees working away from the primary workplace. Where state or local laws contain mandatory requirements that differ from the provisions of this policy, such legal requirements prevail for employees working in affected locations.

3.0 Purpose

To provide another tool for flexible work alternatives to better meet the needs of the company, management, and employees of agcs as well as the environmental concerns of the communities in which we do business.

AGCS anticipates teleworking to benefit AGCS, employees, and the community by:

- better meeting both business and employee needs
- attracting and retaining a diverse and talented workforce
- helping the environment by achieving trip reduction goals as well as decreasing traffic congestion and vehicle emissions to reduce air pollution in all of our business communities

4.0 Definitions

4.1 Casual Teleworker — The casual teleworker has a dedicated office at AGCS and occasionally takes work home. The work completed away from the office may be in addition to the normal work day as assigned, unassigned, or casual overtime or it may be a day selected by the employee based on a management approved teleworking agreement.

4.2 Part-time Teleworker — The part-time teleworker has a dedicated office at AGCS and works from home based upon a management approved teleworking agreement on a routine schedule of 1 or 2 days per week or regularly works overtime at home for a specified period of time.

4.3 Job Demand Teleworker — The job demand teleworker has a dedicated office at AGCS and is required by his or her job situation to work 8 or more non-prime shift hours per week at home.

4.4 Full-time Teleworker — The full-time teleworker does not have an assigned office at AGCS and works primarily from home based upon a management approved teleworking agreement. The full-time teleworker may reserve and use a hoteling office, if available, during periods of work spent at the main offices of AGCS.

4.5 Mobile Teleworker — The mobile teleworker has a dedicated office at AGCS, however he or she has the need to travel on a regular basis and conduct business from a variety of locations using a telephone and/or personal computer and connecting to AGCS systems remotely.

4.6 Satellite Office — Based upon business needs, AGCS may establish satellite offices in other cities convenient to the customer or in areas closer to an available workforce. Marketing sales offices, construction field offices, or neighborhood offices would be defined as satellite offices.

4.7 Hoteling — An unassigned office which is shared by others and is equipped with a workstation and telephone. This office can be reserved by a dedicated teleworker for one or two days while attending to business at the offices of AGCS.

4.8 Teleworking Category Matrix — The level and type of support provided for each type of teleworker is shown on the Teleworking Category Matrix attached to this policy.

5.0 Responsibilities

5.1 Employee responsibilities:

- Become familiar with the Policy and Guidelines for Teleworking, the Teleworking Agreement, and related documents within the *Teleworking Handbook*. The formal Teleworking Agreement is required for all but mobile types of teleworking arrangements.
- Except for those in the casual and mobile categories, potential teleworkers need to complete the Telework Feasibility Survey form, supplied as a part of the *Teleworking Handbook*, to determine if the job and the individual are suited for teleworking.
- Propose the teleworking arrangement to the coach or manager for approval, review with the team if applicable. If the schedule and proposal arc acceptable to both, complete and sign the Teleworking Agreement form and return it to the coach/manager and together review it with the HR and ITS Teleworking Facilitator.
- Become familiar with the Safety and Ergonomic Guidelines in the Teleworking Handbook. Use these guidelines to set up a dedicated work area at home (or other management approved place) that is safe for the employee and others entering it.
- Establish work practices that make teleworking productive for the company and transparent to customers.
- Abide by the terms and conditions of the Teleworking Agreement and teleworking guidelines.
- Report to the office as required for work, meetings, and training at the request of management or customers.
- Safeguard proprietary information and all AGCS assets, including company data in keeping with all AGCS security and computer usage policies and those contained in sections 11.0 and 12.0 of this policy. Failure to comply with these policies will result in loss of teleworking privileges.
- Determine federal, state, and local tax implications resulting from teleworking and satisfy such at their own expense, along with their other personal tax obligations.
- Consult with Safety and Health in setting up an office design.
- Set up work area at home.
- Comply with applicable state and local zoning ordinances.
- Comply with all other terms and conditions of employment.

5.2 Team responsibilities:

- Input to the Telework Feasibility survey, inputting information to assist in the evaluation of the feasibility of teleworking.
- Develop team guidelines on how the team and the teleworker will work together to on a day to day basis, complete projects, and maintain customer satisfaction.
- Communicate with teleworker on a regular basis, including meetings, normal day to day work relations. Teams should make the location of the teleworker transparent to the completion of objectives.

5.3 Coach/Manager responsibilities:

- Become familiar with the Policy and Guidelines for Teleworking, the Teleworking Agreement, and related documents within the *Teleworking Handbook*.
- Encourage and work with employee requests to telework, using the Teleworking Feasibility Survey supplied as a part of the Teleworking Handbook, and implement a teleworking arrangement if beneficial to AGCS business, employees, and the environment. Coach/managers are encouraged to be flexible and give teleworking requests every consideration.
- Make the "business decision" as to whether a request to telework meets the necessary requirements and makes sense from an AGCS perspective. This decision is based on the impact on AGCS, including productivity gains or losses, effect on customer service, employee retention, team and/or department issues and costs.
- Have the employee complete a Teleworking Agreement, file the original in the employee personnel files kept by the coach/manager, and retain for one year after the teleworking arrangement ends. Send a copy of the agreement to the HR Teleworking Facilitator and give the employee a copy for his or her files.
- Update Teleworking Agreement if any aspect of the arrangement covered by the agreement changes, obtain employee's signature, and provide copies as stated in the paragraph immediately above.
- Review computer security and safeguarding of proprietary information with the employee.
- Maintain an accurate inventory, including the location of AGCS owned equipment taken off-site. The employee is required to fill out a High Technology Removal form (FM-44). It should be completed by management and employee when the Teleworking Agreement is finalized. File the yellow copy of FM-44 and retain it for one year after the teleworking arrangement ends.

- Notify Payroll if employee works from a state different than from their AGCS work location state.
- Continue normal management activities including performance appraisals, career development, ongoing feedback, and other normal communications.
- Provide support as required to meet the needs of teleworkers. Meet with the employee on a quarterly basis to assess how it is going and discuss productivity, issues, or difficulties.

5.4 HR Teleworking Facilitator responsibilities:

- Advise and consult with employees and coaches/managers wishing to implement a teleworking arrangement. Work with the Corporate Communications department to communicate teleworking.
- Provide clarification of the teleworking policy and provide advice and training on teleworking practices.
- Answer teleworking questions for both employee and management and provide training to the teleworker, teams or management as required.
- Track the number of teleworkers and evaluate the program for effectiveness.

5.5 ITS Teleworking Facilitator responsibilities:

- Advise and consult with employees and coaches/managers about the technical issues associated with teleworking, including availability of computer hardware, software, and connectivity options.
- Coordinate ITS support for teleworkers.
- Resolve ITS related telework issues.
- Arrange for and coordinate technical training for teleworkers

5.6 Health and Safety representatives will provide consultation or training information on setting up the office using good ergonomic practices.

6.0 Compensation and Benefits

The employee's compensation, benefits, and company sponsored insurance coverage are not affected by the teleworking arrangement.

7.0 Taxes

Employees participating in the teleworking arrangement are responsible for determining federal, state, and local tax implications resulting from working at home and to satisfy each at their own expense along with other personal tax obligations. Employees should refer any tax related questions to their personal tax advisor.

8.0 Hours of Work and Overtime

- An employee's standard work hours are unaffected by the teleworking arrangement. The daily schedule is specified in the Teleworking Agreement.
- The AGCS Overtime policy extends to teleworking arrangements. Refer to HR policy 108, Overtime Compensation, or 129, Overtime Compensation for Nonexempt Employees, for details.

9.0 Safety and Worker's Compensation

- Teleworkers must have work areas designed consistent with sound ergonomic principles and must use safe practices to avoid injury from improper use of equipment. Health and Safety representatives can provide information on design principles.
- Worker's compensation liability for job-related injuries and illnesses and eligibility for accident disability benefits continues during the approved work schedule and in the employee's home work area as described in the Teleworking Agreement. Accidents must be reported to the Health and Safety Department.
- AGCS shall have no liability whatsoever for any injuries to family members, visitors, and others in the employee's home. Employees should consult with their personal insurance carriers for advice.
- Teleworkers are not to hold AGCS business meetings in their home office.

10.0 Disability Benefits

Employees on disability may not be required to work at home during the period of disability benefits. However, if an employee on disability asks to work at home, the manager should consult with the local health and safety representative and follow the medical professional's advice. If approved, the employee's status would change to active from disability.

11.0 Proprietary Information

- The AGCS policy on business and scientific information as specified in HR policy 407 must be followed.
- All AGCS proprietary information must be stored in a locked room, desk, or file cabinet when left unattended. Proprietary information must be disposed of by burning or shredding or must be returned to an AGCS facility for shredding.

12.0 Computers and Security: Protecting AGCS

Depending upon the type of teleworker and the frequency of teleworking, employees may use either company-provided or their own computer equipment to perform their jobs from home. In either case, they must abide by the AGCS policies covering computer security.

12.1 Data protection: AGCS data is a valuable company asset. All teleworkers are responsible for protecting this data. Therefore, data files are to be kept on company network servers, and accessed via the appropriate remote access technology. If it is necessary to move data to a local computer for disconnected work, the teleworker is responsible to update the original at the first opportunity to get remotely connected. Teleworkers are also responsible for backing up their own systems so down time is minimized in the event of system failure. The only copy of company data should not reside exclusively on a remote device. Teleworkers are responsible for making any and all reasonable efforts to back up company data.

12.2 Virus protection: Computer viruses are a fact of life in the computer world. AGCS teleworkers are responsible for insuring that virus protection software from ITS is installed on their systems and enabled. Disabling or removing virus protection systems may result in loss of teleworking privileges. Teleworkers are also responsible for "safe" computing practices, such as avoiding downloads from unfamiliar sources and installing software only from disks provided by a manufacturer or ITS. ITS will maintain online information to assist in this effort and provide current information to the user community.

12.3 Use of company computer assets: AGCS may provide computer software or hardware for teleworkers' use. These assets are for business and not personal use. Software and hardware not licensed to or owned by AGCS may not be installed on AGCS owned computers without approval from ITS. If software is provided to an AGCS employee or contractor for use on a non- AGCS computer, that software must be removed and returned to ITS upon termination of employment or end of contract, or when the software is no longer needed for company use.

12.4 Software Piracy: It is AGCS policy to obtain proper licensing for all software in use on AGCS systems. AGCS employees and contractors are expected to comply with and support this policy. Therefore, all software installed on AGCS owned systems must be properly licensed. Users may not copy or distribute software without authorization from ITS and verification of proper license.

12.5 Use of other technology resources: agcs provides a variety of technology resources, such as e-mail systems and Internet access capability. agcs users are to refrain from using these resources for non-business purposes.

13.0 Company Provided Equipment and Support

Installation of non-AGCS approved software or hardware on AGCS owned equipment will result in loss of teleworking privileges. Company provided equipment is not to be used by non-agcs employees. (i.e., family members, friends, etc.).

13.1 Computer Hardware: AGCS will provide computer hardware assets for teleworkers' use based on the business need and the user's teleworking category (see Teleworker Category Matrix). Details on what can be provided and the necessary approval information can be found in the ITS Hardware Policy document.

13.2 Software: AGCS will provide computer software for teleworkers' use based on the business need and the user's teleworking category (see Teleworker Category Matrix, section 2 of the AGCS *Teleworking Handbook*). Software installation disks may be provided on a loan basis. The user is responsible for returning loaner disks by the time agreed to when the disks are checked out. Hardcopy documentation may not be provided, or may be available at additional cost billable to the user's department. Details on what can be provided and the necessary approval information can be found in the ITS Software Policy document.

13.3 Operating Systems: AGCS does not provide operating systems software for computer systems that are not owned by the company. A teleworker who will be using a personal system must provide a company approved desktop OS in order to receive support from the help desk. Currently approved and supported operating systems may be found in the ITS Operating System Policy document.

14.0 If Employee Owned Computer Systems Are Used:

➤ Any computer hardware expenses (to include maintenance, repairs, and insurance) are the employee's responsibility. Certain items such as modems may be provided at the discretion of ITS.

- Company data must be kept in separate directories or folders. It must be regularly backed up on removable computing media clearly marked as AGCS property (see section 12.1).
- Any software used for AGCS company business must be properly licensed. Only properly licensed software may be installed on a system used for an AGCS network.
- All agcs information and AGCS network connections must be secured before leaving the work area. The employee is responsible for providing the same protection of company proprietary information at home as they do while working at the AGCS office.

15.0 Expenses

15.1 Reimbursable Expenses — Any reimbursable expenses must be authorized by the coach/manager and charged to the employee's department or project.

The Teleworking Agreement will specify expenses that the coach/manager may have authorized for reimbursement. For example, installation of a second telephone line and monthly fees may be approved by the manager as a reimbursable expense. To be reimbursed for other business expenses that may arise, the employee should seek management approval before incurring them. As needed, basic office supplies such as paper, pens, and clips will be provided by AGCS for the teleworker.

Reasonable travel expenses may be authorized by the coach/manager for dedicated long distance teleworkers to return to the main offices of AGCS for meetings.

15.2 Non-reimbursable Expenses: Examples of non-reimbursable expenses are included in the following list. This list is not all inclusive; the coach/manager and the teleworking coordinator will confer and make any individual determination as required.

- Any costs related to remodeling and furnishing the home work space. The teleworker must insure that they have space that can provide a productive, safe work environment.
- Local commuting expenses between the work location and the regular AGCS work location.
- All household related expenses such as rent (or mortgage payments), heating, and electricity.
- Cost of insurance purchased purely for the teleworker's protection or benefit.

16.0 Termination of Teleworking Agreement

The teleworking agreement may be terminated at any time for any reason by the employee or manager. However, employees or managers wanting to terminate a teleworking agreement should discuss the request with one another at least 30 calendar days before terminating the arrangement. Notwithstanding the above, AGCS may modify or terminate a Teleworking Agreement and arrangement at any time for any reason.

When the Teleworking Agreement is terminated, at management request, or when employment is terminated, all AGCS owned computer equipment, disks, and documentation must be returned to ITS, and all AGCS licensed software removed from non-AGCS owned systems.

17.0 Teleworking Handbook & Documents

The *Teleworking Handbook* contains guidelines, documents, and forms which are to be used with this policy. Signing the Teleworking Agreement does not affect the employee's employment status. The employee remains employed not by contract, but at will, meaning the employee and AGCS are each free to terminate the employment relationship at any time for any reason.

Appendix 3
TELECOMMUTER'S AGREEMENT

Sample Telecommuter's Agreement
California Department of Personnel Administration (www.dpa.ca.gov)

Both the manager and the telecommuter understand that home based telecommuting is a bilateral voluntary option and can be discontinued at either's request with no adverse repercussions.

The (agency) will pay for the following expenses:

- Charges for business related telephone calls
- Maintenance and repairs to state owned equipment

Claims will be submitted on a Travel Expense Claim along with receipt, bill, or other verification of the expense.

The (agency) will not pay for the following expenses:

- Maintenance or repairs of privately owned equipment
- Utility costs associated with the use of the computer or occupation of the home
- Equipment supplies (these should be requisitioned through the main office)
- Travel expenses (other than authorized transit subsidies) associated with commuting to the central office

Telecommute days are scheduled and will not be substituted without advance approval of the manager. In the office days will be ______________. Home office days will be ______________.

Telecommuters must be available by phone during the core business hours of _______to _______.

Use of sick leave, vacation, time off, or other leave credits must be approved in advance by the supervisor. Overtime to be worked must be approved in advance by the supervisor.

Telecommuting is not a substitute for dependent care and telecommuters must make regular dependent care arrangements.

The telecommuter has read and understands the agency's telecommuting policies and agrees to abide by those policies.

The telecommuter is to carry out the steps needed for good information security in the home office setting and has a copy of the agency's security requirements and procedures. The telecommuter agrees to check with her or his supervisor when security matters are an issue.

______________________________ ______________________________
(Supervisor) (Date) (Telecommuter) (Date)

Appendix 4
TELECOMMUTING AGREEMENT

US Office of Personnel Management
Sample Telecommuting Agreement

(Agencies may use or modify this sample agreement)

Between Agency and Employee Approved for Telecommuting on a Continuing Basis

The supervisor and the employee should each keep a copy of the agreement for reference.

Voluntary Participation

Employee voluntarily agrees to work at the agency approved alternative workplace indicated below and to follow all applicable policies and procedures. Employee recognizes that the telecommuting arrangement is not an employee entitlement but an additional method the agency may approve to accomplish work.

Trial Period

Employee and agency agree to try out the arrangement for at least (specify number) months unless unforeseeable difficulties require earlier cancellation.

Salary and Benefits

Agency agrees that a telecommuting arrangement is not a basis for changing the employee's salary or benefits.

Duty Station and Alternative Workplace

Agency and employee agree that the employee's official duty station is (indicate duty station for regular office) and that the employee's approved alternative workplace is: (specify street and number, city, and state).

Note: All pay, leave, and travel entitlement are based on the official duty station.

Official Duties

Unless otherwise instructed, employee agrees to perform official duties only at the regular office or agency-approved alternative workplace. Employee agrees not to conduct personal business while in official duty status at the alternative workplace, for example, caring for dependents or making home repairs.

Work Schedule and Tour of Duty

Agency and employee agree the employee's official tour of duty will be: (specify days, hours, and location, i.e., the regular office or the alternative workplace. For flexible work schedules, specify core hours and the limits within which flexible hours may be worked).

Time and Attendance

Agency agrees to make sure the telecommuting employee's timekeeper has a copy of the employee's work schedule. The supervisor agrees to certify biweekly the time and attendance for hours worked at the regular office and the alternative workplace. (Note: Agency may require employee to complete self-certification form.)

Leave

Employee agrees to follow established office procedures for requesting and obtaining approval of leave.

Overtime

Employee agrees to work overtime only when ordered and approved by the supervisor in advance and understands that overtime work without such approval is not compensated and may result in termination of the telecommuting privilege and/or other appropriate action.

Equipment/Supplies

Employee agrees to protect any government-owned equipment and to use the equipment only for official purposes. The agency agrees to install, service, and maintain any government-owned equipment issued to the telecommuting employee. The employee agrees to install, service, and maintain any personal equipment used. The agency agrees to provide the employee with all necessary office supplies and also reimburse the employee for business-related long distance telephone calls.

Security

If the government provides computer equipment for the alternative workplace, employee agrees to the following security provisions: (insert agency-specific language).

Liability

The employee understands that the government will not be liable for damages to an employee's personal or real property while the employee is working at the approved alternative workplace, except to the extent the government is held liable by the Federal Tort Claims Act or the Military Personnel and Civilian Employees Claims Act.

Work Area

The employee agrees to provide a work area adequate for performance of official duties.

Worksite Inspection

The employee agrees to permit the government to inspect the alternative workplace during the employee's normal working hours to ensure proper maintenance of government-owned property and conformance with safety standards. (Agencies may require employees to complete a self-certification safety checklist.)

Alternative Workplace Costs

The employee understands that the government will not be responsible for any operating costs that are associated with the employee using his or her home as an alternative worksite, for example, home maintenance, insurance, or utilities. The employee understands he or she does not relinquish any entitlement to reimbursement for authorized expenses incurred while conducting business for the government, as provided for by statute and regulations.

Injury Compensation

Employee understands he or she is covered under the Federal Employee's Compensation Act if injured in the course of actually performing official duties at the regular office or the alternative duty station. The employee agrees to notify the supervisor immediately of any accident or injury that occurs at the alternative workplace and to complete any required forms. The supervisor agrees to investigate such a report immediately.

Work Assignments/Performance

Employee agrees to complete all assigned work according to procedures mutually agreed upon by the employee and the supervisor and according to guidelines and standards in the employee performance plan. The employee agrees to provide regular reports if required by the supervisor to help judge performance. The employee understands that a decline in performance may be grounds for canceling the alternative workplace arrangement.

Disclosure

Employee agrees to protect government/agency records from unauthorized disclosure or damage and will comply with requirements of the Privacy Act of 1974, 5 USC 552a.

Standards of Conduct

Employee agrees he or she is bound by agency standards of conduct while working at the alternative worksite.

Cancellation

Agency agrees to let the employee resume his or her regular schedule at the regular office after notice to the supervisor. Employee understands that the agency may cancel the telecommuting arrangement and instruct the employee to resume working at the regular office. The agency agrees to follow any applicable administrative or negotiated procedures.

Other Action

Nothing in this agreement precludes the agency from taking any appropriate disciplinary or adverse action against an employee who fails to comply with the provisions of this agreement.

Employee's Signature and Date: ______________________________

Supervisor's Signature and Date: ______________________________

(US Office of Personnel Management, <www.opm.gov>)

Appendix 5
TELECOMMUTING RESOURCES

4anything.com Telecommuting

http://4telecommuting.4anything.com/?%3B002002a

4anything.com's Telecommuting resource site provides links and information on every aspect of telecommuting. The site serves as a portal to an enormous amount of information and links to associations, articles, and other resources.

About.com Telecommuting

http://telecommuting.about.com/smallbusiness/telecommuting/mbody.htm

This About.com guide offers a wealth of information, frequently updated, on telecommuting. It includes sample agreements, information on conferences and events, facts and figures, as well as helpful home office tips, technology information, and links to telecommuting jobs.

AT&T Telework Guide

www.att.com/telework/

AT&T shares messages from the trenches — articles on real people doing real work using real technology and having real experiences. AT&T has had a formal telework program in place since 1992. The site offers practical tools, based on their experience, to help others get started, as well as links to AT&T products and services, and more.

Canadian Telework Association

www.ivc.ca/

The Canadian Telework Association (CTA) is a Canadian nonprofit telework association dedicated to promoting telework in Canada. Members include individuals, corporate bodies (small, medium, and large), academics, and governments (at all levels). They come from dozens of countries.

Gil Gordon Associates

www.gilgordon.com

Operating since May 1995, this site consolidates a wide variety of information from around the world, and from many different perspectives, on the subjects of telecommuting, teleworking, the virtual office, and related topics. The site has been honored by several awards, including the Site Selection Insider's Web Pick of the Week award. Gil Gordon is an acknowledged expert in the implementation of telecommuting and telework.

ITAC (International Telework Association and Council)

www.telecommute.org

ITAC is a nonprofit organization dedicated to promoting the benefits of teleworking. The site offers information about the design and implementation of teleworking programs, the development of the US telework sector, and research.

JALA

www.jala.com

JALA is an international group of management consultants that was incorporated in California in 1982

Their activities are in four main areas:

- Telework, telecommuting, and virtual offices (JALA is a virtual firm)
- Applied futures research and forecasting
- Technology assessment
- Regional telecommunications planning

The Web site is designed to inform visitors and to demonstrate and enhance the services JALA provides to future and current clients. They've provided a number of resources to help visitors learn more about them, telework, and the future.

Smart Valley Telecommuting guide

http://smartone.svi.org/PROJECTS/TCOMMUTE/TCGUIDE/

The Smart Valley Telecommuting Guide and the results of the Smart Valley Telecommuting pilot project are available online in a variety of formats and languages.

Telecommute now!

www.telecommuting.com

TeleCommuting.Com Inc. manages a collaborative environment between corporations worldwide and potential employees that prefer to work from the comfort of their own homes. Their Knowledge Center promotes and demonstrates the increasing importance and exigency for telecommuting by educating potential users of telecommuting technologies. The site offers information, links, and lists the latest events surrounding telecommuting and the implementation of telecommuting technologies.

Telecommuting Knowledge Center

www.telecommuting.org

The Telecommuting Knowledge Center (TKC) is the most comprehensive online sourcebook and information center for telecommuting technologies. TKC participants have access to an extensive resource of telecommuting literature, vendors, consultants, products, services, and events. All of these items have been categorized to make it easy to research specific telecommuting topics.